# Religions and Beliefs

## Series Editor: Ina Taylor

# Judaism

Nelson Thornes

Published in 2006 by:
Nelson Thornes Ltd
Delta Place
27 Bath Road
CHELTENHAM
GL53 7TH
United Kingdom

08 09 10 / 10 9 8 7 6 5 4 3 2 1

A catalogue record for this book is available from the British Library

ISBN 978 0 7487 9671 7

Edited by Judi Hunter
Picture research by Sue Sharp
Illustrations by Angela Lumley and Harry Venning
Page make-up by eMC Design

Printed in Croatia by Zrinski

**Acknowledgements**
With thanks to the following for permission to reproduce photographs and other copyright
material in this book:

Cover photo: Uzi Yachin

Alamy/ Paul Bricknell: 53B; Alamy/ Israel Images/ Israel Talby: 31B; Alamy/ Chris Rout: 32A;
Andes Press Agency/ Carlos Reyes Manzo: 52A; ArkReligion.com/ Art Directors & Trip Photo
Library/ Helene Rogers:  22A, 38A, 55C; Bridgeman Art Library 'Adam and Eve' design (w/c on
paper), Voysey, Charles Francis Annesley (1857–1941)/ Private Collection, The Stapleton
Collection: 50A; Keith Brofsky/ Photodisc 40 (NT): 43 (right); CIRCA Photo Library: 8B; Corbis/
Dider Bauweraerts/ Van Parys Media: 13B; Corbis/ Bettman: 51C; Corbis/ Yves Herman/
Reuters: 43 (bottom); Corbis/ images.com: 24; Corbis/ Jim Holland/ EPA: 5; Corbis/ Ramin
Talaie: 32C; Getty Images: 43 (top left); Getty/ Guy Edwardes: 62; Greater Manchester Police:
41C; House of Lords/ Lord Janner of Braunstone: 39B; Israelimages.com/ Sammy Avnisan: 17C;
Jewish Child's Day: 47B; Jewish Council for Racial Equality: 45D; Jewish Telegraph, reproduced
by courtesy of the Jewish Telegraph Group of Newspapers: 40A & B; The Maimonides
Foundation: 61B & C; Manchester Jewish Museum: 7C; Daniel Beder: 34A; Nature Picture
Library/ Nick Turner: 54B; The Noah Project: 54A; Barbara Penoyar/ Photodisc 16 (NT): 35B;
Lawrence Purcell/ Jewish Chronicle: 60A; Reuters: 39C; Rex Features: 44A; Rex Features/ Sipa
Press: 29C, 57C; Rex Features/ Justin Williams: 23B; Sonia Halliday Photographs: 10A, 27C;
Steve Allen Photography: 15C; Still Pictures/ Johannes Schmid/ Das Fotoarchiv: 13C; Ina Taylor:
14B, 16B, 18A, 25, 30A, 46A, 56A, 58A, 59B; Tzedek: 48; The Union of Jewish Students: 37C;
University Jewish Chaplaincy Board: 36B; World Jewish Relief: 49; ZAKA: 11B.

Extracts on pages 22, 33D and 59 taken from the website of the Chief Rabbi,
www.chiefrabbi.org, and reproduced with kind permission of the Office of the Chief Rabbi.

Extracts on pages 29 and 40 taken from the *Jewish Telegraph* (30/09/05 and 23/09/05,
respectively), and reproduced by courtesy of the Jewish Telegraph Group of Newspapers.

Extract on page 41 taken from the website of the Jewish Council for Racial Equality (JCORE),
www.jcore.org.uk, and reproduced with kind permission.

Scriptures are taken from the *Good News Bible* published by The Bible Societies/Collins
© American Bible Society.

Every effort has been made to contact copyright holders. The publishers apologise to anyone
whose rights have been inadvertently overlooked, and will be happy to rectify any errors or
omissions.

# Contents

 # Fast facts about Judaism

**Q When did it begin?**

Judaism is the second oldest of the six major world religions and began approximately 4,000 years ago in the region of Mesopotamia, which is where modern-day Iraq is. Abraham is considered to be the father of the Jewish people and Moses the father of the Jewish faith.

**Q What is Judaism?**

It is the name of the religion followed by the Jewish people. Some people are Jewish because they are born into a Jewish family but they may not regard themselves as religious Jews because they do not follow the religious way of life.

**Q Are there different types of Judaism?**

As in any religion, there are various types of Judaism. The main ones in the UK are Orthodox, Reform and Liberal. Orthodox Jews closely follow the teachings and traditions of the faith, Reform and Liberal Jews have adapted their faith to the modern world.

**Q How many Jewish people are there in the world today?**

Judaism is the smallest of the six major world religions with about 12 million followers in the world, most of whom live in Israel and the USA. In the UK, there are approximately 268,000 Jewish people, about 85,000 of these would call themselves religious Jews.

# Looking for meaning

It often helps to talk something through with another person. Not only can you learn from them, but it can help you to understand an issue when you have to explain it to someone else. These Jewish young men are discussing the meaning of a passage of scripture. They are students at a yeshiva, which is a Jewish college any adult Jewish male can attend.

- What lessons have you had where you have found it useful to work with a partner?
- Why did it work well on that occasion?
- What advantages do you think this method of study has when the subject is a religion?

5

# Beliefs about God

## glossary

Creator
Free will
Orthodox Jew
Shema
Ten
   Commandments

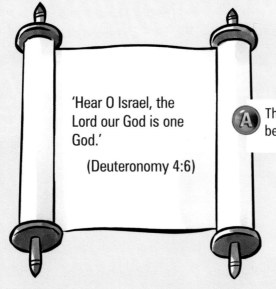

'Hear O Israel, the Lord our God is one God.'

(Deuteronomy 4:6)

**A** This is the most important belief in Judaism – the **Shema**.

God gives people **free will** – We are free to decide whether or not we follow the rules that God sets. Those who do will be rewarded, and those who do not will be punished.

God the **creator** – God made everything that exists, the earth, the planets and all the universes. God made them out of nothing. God continues to create every single day as new life appears on earth. 'In the beginning, when God created the universe, the earth was formless and desolate' (Genesis 1:1).

God knows everything – God knows what happened in the past. He knows exactly what is going on everywhere at the moment and what will happen in the future.

God cares – God looks after his creation. He provides everything it needs to survive. He loves and protects the people he made.

**B** **One God – There is only one God who cannot be divided into parts like a father or a son.**

God gives people rules to live by – God has shown people the correct way to lead their lives.

God is a spirit – God does not have a body or gender like us, although it is customary to refer to God as He, using a capital letter as a sign of respect. God is a spirit that is everywhere and in everything. His greatness can be seen in the wonders of nature. 'His glory fills the world' (Isaiah 6:3).

God is powerful – God can make things happen if he wants to. He is stronger than anything else that has ever existed or ever will exist.

God has revealed himself to humanity – This happened once in ancient times when God descended on to Mount Sinai.

God is outside of time – Nothing made God because he had no beginning. He will not die because he has no end. God is active in the world today.

Diagram **B** shows the basic Jewish beliefs about God. Any one of these ideas is mind-blowing! When they are all put together, it is very hard to get an idea of God in your mind.

Jews believe that, although God is a unique and powerful being, it is still possible for people to have a personal relationship with him. They believe they can get closer to God through prayer and reading the words he handed down to them in the holy scriptures.

It is important to remember that Jews believe God is such a holy being that it is wrong to attempt to draw pictures of him. For some Jews, it is also offensive to even write his name in full, so you may well come across 'G-d' in some books. This is because books are written on paper which can easily be destroyed or thrown away. **Orthodox Jews**, who follow God's rules as closely as possible, believe treating a piece of paper with the name of God on in that way is deeply offensive. You can probably understand this view if you think how upset you would be if a photograph of someone you cared deeply about was thrown in the mud and stamped on.

> **Activity**
>
> 1   Design a poster to display some of the different aspects of God given on these pages. To do this without causing offence to Orthodox Jews you will need to use symbols that represent these different aspects. You could draw them or cut them out of a magazine. For instance, you might choose a picture of hands cradling something as an example of God caring.
>
> 2   What *three* questions would you like to e-mail to God who knows everything?
>
> 3   Imagine you are in charge of a school. You have the power to make rules; to put pupils in detention or exclude them; and to sack teachers who do not do their job properly. Describe what sort of head teacher you would be and how your school would be run.

This is a stained-glass window from a synagogue in Manchester. It portrays the story of the travelling Ark of the Covenant but you will notice that God is not depicted in the picture. It is forbidden in the **Ten Commandments** to make any images of God.

# Beliefs about humanity

It says in Genesis, the first book of the Bible, that God created everything in six days. It also describes how on the final day, 'God created human beings, making them to be like himself' (Genesis 1:27). Humans were the highest point of God's creation and he was pleased with them. When it says humans are like God, Jews do not think this means people actually look like God. They think it means everyone has a spark of God within them and is capable of doing great things.

**A** 'What are human beings, that you think of them; mere mortals, that you care for them?

Yet you made them inferior only to yourself; you crowned them with glory and honour.

You appointed them rulers over everything you made...'

(Psalm 8:4–6)

**B** This small box is a **mezuzah** case which is fixed to the door of a Jewish home. It contains a piece of parchment with the Shema prayer on it (you can read part of the Shema on page 30). The mezuzah symbolises the close link between God and his people.

One important gift Jews believe God gave people was free will. This means people can choose what they do. As the great Jewish teacher **Moses Maimonides** explained:

Man has been given free will: if he wishes to turn towards the good way and to be righteous, the power is in his own hands; if he wishes to turn towards the evil way and to be wicked, the power is likewise in his own hands.

To help people lead the sort of life that God wants, seven basic rules were handed down in ancient times. They are called the **Noahide Laws** because God gave them to Noah after the flood. These are considered basic rules that everyone on earth should live by, no matter what their religion. Later, God gave the Jews more detailed rules.

The Bible makes it clear that everyone was created by God. This means everyone is equal no matter what race, colour or religion they are.

The book of Genesis also describes how God put humans in charge of the world telling them:

'Have many children, so that your descendants will live all over the earth and bring it under their control.'

(Genesis 1:28)

Controlling the planet sounds a huge responsibility for humanity but Jews believe we are not on our own. They say we are partners with God in caring for the world.

1  Complete a piece of writing that starts: 'If I ruled the world…'

2  It is easy to think of ways in which we harm the planet, but can you name *two* projects which bring good to the earth?

3  Plan *seven* basic rules that you think would make a good school, no matter what type of school it is.

4  What does the psalmist, whose words appear in **A**, say about the position of people in God's creation?

# The Covenant

Jews believe that, although God is powerful, he made a special agreement with humanity. It is like striking a deal with someone. Each side agrees to do something; it is a two-way thing. In order to show both sides have agreed on the terms, people often shake hands.

The special deal God made with the Jews is called the **Covenant**. Below is what each side promised.

God promised:

- to look after the Jews
- to make them his chosen people
- to give them the land of Canaan, now called Israel.

The Jews promised:

- to love God
- to keep his commandments.

# The sign

In order to show they agreed with the terms God set out, the Jews were asked to circumcise all their males. This is a simple operation which involves removing the foreskin of the penis. It is still carried out today when a baby boy is eight days old.

The relationship between Jewish people and God is central to their religion. Jews do not think they are better than anyone else, it is simply that God has chosen them to have special responsibilities and these are not easy ones.

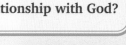

**D** A deal is a two-way agreement. People often shake hands as a sign they agree to the deal. The Covenant is an agreement between God and the Jews. Circumcision is the sign Jews agree with it.

5  When Jews pray they often address God as 'Our Father, our King'. What does this show about their relationship with God?

# Put it in writing

We all find it reassuring to have somewhere we can turn to when we need advice. A wise person can be extremely helpful but they may not be there when you need them. There is also the problem that they are human and will die. It is also possible that as they get older they become unreliable, forget or change their mind and offer conflicting advice. For those reasons, most of us like to have things in writing. It's reliable and we can look back at the information when we need to. This is one reason why the **Torah**, the Jews' holiest writings, is held in such high regard.

The Torah is the name given to the first five books of the Bible: Genesis; Exodus; Leviticus; Numbers; and Deuteronomy. In a **synagogue**, these five books will be handwritten on one parchment scroll called the **Sefer Torah**, this literally means 'scroll of the Torah'. A synagogue is likely to own more than one Sefer Torah and probably scrolls with other books of the Bible written on them. All the scrolls will be kept in the **ark**. This special cupboard is the holiest part of the synagogue because it contains the word of God.

## objective

to understand the importance of the Torah to Jews

## glossary

Ark
Liberal Jew
Mantle
Reform Jew
Sefer Torah
Synagogue
Tallit
Torah

(A) Everyone must give their full attention to the Torah when it is being read in the synagogue. For these Jewish soldiers, a tent has become their synagogue but the Torah receives the same respect.

When the Torah is taken out of the ark to be read, it is carried high with great respect and ceremony. The congregation faces the scroll as it passes, and some reach out a tassel of their **tallit** to touch the **mantle** that covers the scrolls, and then kiss the tassel to show their love for God's word.

## The word of God

Orthodox Jews believe the Torah was given to them by God (see pages 20–21). The words are those revealed by God directly to Moses and handed on carefully to his successors. Since then, great care in copying has ensured no mistake has crept in, so the Torah is believed to be word for word the same as it was in Moses' time.

The Torah is important proof of God's relationship with the Jews and records the history of God working with them. The Torah also contains instructions from God about how Jews should lead their lives. These are written instructions which people can refer to at any time in history because the instructions will last forever. It is the Torah that unites the Jewish people and sets the standard for their behaviour.

Jews from the **Liberal** and **Reform** traditions are not convinced the Torah contains the exact words spoken by God. They believe that some teachings in the Torah never go out of date but other teachings only apply to the time when the Torah was written. However, the scriptures in the Torah form the basis of their beliefs and remain central to the way they lead their lives.

'Study it [the Torah] again and again, for everything is in it. Contemplate it, grow old and grey in it, and do not stir from it, for you can have no better guide in life than it.'

(Ethics of the Fathers)

**B** ## SCROLLS RESCUED FROM NEW ORLEANS FLOOD

Volunteer rescue worker, Isaac Leider, set out in a boat with four members of the National Guard to rescue scrolls from a Louisiana synagogue after hurricane Katrina. Once in the synagogue, Isaac waded waist-deep through the flood waters to get the six scrolls out of the ark. They were blackened with toxic water and badly damaged, but saved. Sadly, only two are fit to be restored.

**C** An elderly rabbi in a Nazi death camp was ordered to take off his clothes by a guard. He refused. The guards began beating him with wooden clubs but still he refused. As he lay unconscious and bleeding on the ground, the guards forced other Jews to remove his clothing. Only then did they discover that the rabbi had wrapped a Torah scroll around his body to keep it safe.

The incident in **C** shows how some Jews are prepared to face death rather than be separated from the word of God.

**Activity**

1  One Jewish scholar said the Torah was the essence of Judaism. How could that be true?

2  Make a leaflet to give to synagogue visitors to explain the importance of the Torah scrolls.

3  Describe an object that is of great personal value to you, even though it may not be worth a lot of money. Explain why it has great personal significance for you.

4  Role-play a television interview with Isaac Leider. Viewers will be interested to know why Isaac made such efforts to rescue these scrolls.

# People in authority

### glossary

Bet Din
Halakhah
Ketuvim
Kosher
Matriarch
Nevi'im
Patriarch
Prophet
Rabbi
Tenakh

## The patriarchs

Abraham, Isaac and Jacob were the first men chosen by God to be the founding fathers of Judaism, these are the **patriarchs**. Their wives, known as the **matriarchs**, are regarded as the mothers of the Jewish people. By using the patriarchs to tell people the standard of behaviour God wanted and to accept the terms of his Covenant, God was conferring divine authority on them to be leaders.

A As you can see from this diagram, people do play an important part in Judaism. The triangle shows that this religion relies on three things to succeed. If you take any one away, Judaism will collapse.

GOD

JUDAISM

PEOPLE                    TORAH

## The prophets

Many years later, God chose Moses to be a **prophet** (in other words a messenger) and God gave Moses the Torah on Mount Sinai. Moses was an ordinary person who was empowered by God to lead the people.

Years afterwards, when the Jews began to neglect the Covenant they had agreed with God, other prophets appeared. These men were directly inspired by God to lead the Jews back from their pagan ways to obey the terms of the Covenant they had agreed with God. The prophets knew exactly how God wanted people to live and they were not scared to stand up and shout at those who disobeyed, no matter how unpopular it made them!

The lives and teachings of the prophets were written down and form a significant part of the Hebrew Bible which is called the **TeNaKh**. **T** is the Torah element; **N** is the **Nevi'im**, which are the writings of the Prophets; and **K** is the **Ketuvim**, which are the rest of the writings.

## The rabbis

When the Romans destroyed the Temple in Jerusalem in 70 CE the focal point of Jewish worship came to an end. Although the building had gone and the priests dispersed, the Torah remained as the heart of the religion. A group of scholars and teachers grew up whose detailed knowledge of the Torah enabled them to help people understand the meaning of God's word.

These people were the **rabbis** who took over from the prophets and the priests as the source of human authority in Judaism. With the rabbis came synagogues, which were places where Jews could meet and learn about their religion as well as worship together.

1 Describe the different ways God has communicated his message to the Jews throughout history.

# Modern rabbis

The role of rabbis has changed little in 2,000 years. They have a good knowledge of the Torah and the **Halakhah** (which is the Jewish law based on the Torah), so they are able to help members of their community live the way God requires. It is usual for a rabbi today to have a university degree followed by a further five years study at a rabbinical college. Only then it is thought the person will have sufficient knowledge and authority to be ordained as a rabbi.

In Orthodox Judaism, which follows the traditional ways of the religion, only men can become rabbis, whereas Liberal and Reform Judaism permit women rabbis.

All the different branches of Judaism have their own leader. Orthodox Jews in Britain are led by the Chief Rabbi, Dr Jonathan Sacks. Although the Liberal and Reform Jewish movements in Britain also have their own leaders, the Chief Rabbi often speaks on behalf of all British Jews.

A rabbi may be a member of the **Bet Din**, the Jewish court of three rabbis with the authority to rule on matters of Jewish law. Their duties include checking to see whether food is **kosher**; deciding whether a Jewish couple are permitted a divorce; and checking whether a person is suitably prepared for conversion to Judaism.

B In 2005, the first female rabbi was appointed in Belgium. Thirty-one-year-old Floriane Chinsky was born in Paris, then studied and was ordained in Jerusalem before her appointment to the Reform synagogue in Brussels. She is now the leading Liberal rabbi in that country.

C The man on the right is a member of the Bet Din. He is checking on the production of kosher wine.

2 What are the advantages of having a person in authority?

3 a What advantages might there be in having a young woman as a leader?

b What would an Orthodox Jew say about those points?

13

# Getting closer to God

Putting God's will into practice is at the heart of Jewish spirituality. It is also what Jews agreed to do when they accepted the Covenant with God (pages 8–9 will remind you of the Covenant). Jews believe God has a divine plan for the whole universe and they must work with God to implement this plan on earth. Everything a person does in their life contributes to the plan and, at the same time, helps that person's own spiritual development.

**A** 'The Holy One, blessed be He, wanted to give Israel the opportunity to win merit; He therefore gave them copious Torah and many commandments, as it is said, it pleased the Lord for the sake of [Israel's] righteousness to make the Torah great and glorious.'

(Ethics of the Fathers)

## Torah study

Because Orthodox Jews believe the Torah is God's word, study of the scriptures will help them to understand what God wants from them. This, in turn, will bring them closer to God. Studying and learning the Torah is only one part of it though. In order to keep their side of the Covenant, Jews have to put the Torah into action in their daily lives.

**Activity**

1 Why does the quotation in **A** say the Torah has so many rules in it? Do you think these would help a Jew or scare them? Why?

## Prayer

Communicating with God through prayer is another spiritual activity that can bring a person closer to God. It does not matter whether that prayer is part of a daily ritual or something that comes into a person's mind spontaneously. All are ways of communicating directly with God and can make that person more open to God's reply.

**B** These pieces of silverwork are extremely ornate and used to decorate the outside of the Torah scrolls. The precious metals and fabrics that have been used, along with the care that has been lavished on the craftsmanship, show how much the Torah is valued by Jews.

# Obeying the mitzvot

A **mitzvah** is an action commanded by God and written down in the holy scriptures. This means that obeying the **mitzvot** (the plural of mitzvah) must be the highest priority for Orthodox Jews who try to follow the Torah as closely as possible. Carrying out God's commands is a spiritual experience because it brings a person closer to God.

> 'The Lord rewards me because I do what is right;
>
> He blesses me because I am innocent.
>
> I have obeyed the law of the Lord;
>
> I have not turned away from my God.
>
> I have observed all his laws;
>
> I have not disobeyed his commands.'
>
> (Psalm 18:20–22)

2 How can a Jew get closer to God?

3 Why is the Torah central to Jewish spirituality?

4 Write your own story based on the phrase: 'Actions speak louder than words'.

5 a What symbols can you identify in the stained-glass window in **C**? Write the meanings each would have for a Jewish person. Make sure you research the symbols you do not know.

  b Can you remember why the name of God, which appears in Hebrew in the blue glass towards the top of the window, has been deliberately masked on this page?

  c Do you think a window like this aids spirituality or is a distraction to worshippers? Why?

  d When you are learning something at school, which do you prefer: a diagram; a written explanation; or the teacher talking about the concept? Try to include some real life examples in your answer.

C This stained-glass window is in the holiest part of the synagogue, above the ark. Some people find that looking at, and thinking about, a work of art can be a spiritual experience. It can help them comprehend ideas that are difficult to put into words.

# The channel of communication

Today, we are only too aware of the usefulness of phones. How did people manage in the past without a mobile? It enables you to pass information to a friend and listen to what they have to say in return. For Jews, prayer plays a similar role. It enables them to speak to God and also to hear what God has to say to them.

Prayer does not have to be an elaborate public display. In the Bible, Hannah was praised for the quiet way she prayed:

'She was praying silently; her lips were moving, but she made no sounds.'

(1 Samuel 1:13)

What parts of her behaviour do you think show that her prayer was sincere?

There are different ways in which a Jew can pray.

1  It is a mitzvah, which means it is commanded by God, that Jewish men pray three times a day: morning; afternoon; and evening. (When possible, prayer should be said facing Jerusalem, where the ancient Temple stood.) Some believe having set times is good otherwise people would forget their prayer duty completely.

2  Little prayers, or blessings, can be said at any time. They are like an instant thank you to God for his goodness. It might be a blessing for food, or a beautiful sunny day or the sight of a rose. Plenty of people today who do not belong to any religion are likely to say, 'O bless' when confronted with something lovely like a little baby or a kind action.

3  A Jew might suddenly feel the need to ask for God's help, want to show their thanks to God or may need to pour out their worries in a friendly ear. This could produce a spontaneous prayer.

**A** These women are praying at the Western Wall, the holiest place for Jews. Not only have they chosen to say their prayers, but some have wedged tiny pieces of paper with prayers on in the crevices. Why would they do this?

1 Draw a diagram of Jewish prayer. Things you need to include are the two-way nature of prayer, as well as different types of prayer.

2 Role-play an interview between a Jew and a Christian about the advantages and problems of having set prayers at set times.

# Group strength

You have only got to be one of the supporters at a football match to know how good it feels to be with a group. Not only do you get a buzz, but your understanding and enjoyment of the activity is heightened. It was set down in earlier times that 10 adult Jewish males needed to meet before communal prayer could take place. These 10 are called the **minyan**. Only when there is a minyan can certain prayers be recited and passages of scripture read in the synagogue.

**B** A Jewish man dressed for morning prayer. Orthodox women do not wear these prayer garments and can pray at times that fit in with their family duties.

# Getting in the right mood

Everyone knows what it is like when somebody says sorry in an off-hand way that clearly shows they don't mean it. It's worthless and insulting. They might as well not have bothered. For the words to have any value they have got to be said sincerely.

Prayer is no different. Jews are aware that God knows what is going on in their minds and prayers chanted for the sake of it are a waste of everyone's time. They are worthless. A Jewish person must put their mind to the task, be intensely aware of God and concentrate on the prayer. How else will they be able to receive God's answer?

To help them get in the right frame of mind, Jewish men put on prayer garments. On the head, a cap called a **kippah** is worn to show respect for God and a prayer shawl, called a tallit, is put around the shoulders. Some say the tallit helps them to feel they are wrapping the love of God around them. On the man's forehead and left arm are wrapped ceremonial leather straps called **tefillin**. Two small boxes contain tiny pieces of parchment with the Shema written on them (see page 6). The box on the forehead helps the man focus his thoughts on loving God with all his mind. The tefillin on the arm is worn with the box close to the heart as a sign that the man loves God with all his strength.

3 Choose *two* outfits and describe how different they make you feel when you wear them. (Tip: Choose a sports outfit and something formal to make this an easier task!)

# Get on with life!

'I believe with perfect faith that there will be a resurrection of the dead at the time when it will please the Creator, blessed be His Name.'

Above is one of the 13 Principles of the Jewish Faith.

'Blessed are You, Lord, who renews life beyond death.'

This is part of the Amidah prayer a Jew says every day.

## objective

to think about different Jewish ideas about life after death

## glossary

Messiah
Reincarnation
Resurrection

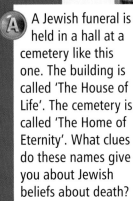

**A** A Jewish funeral is held in a hall at a cemetery like this one. The building is called 'The House of Life'. The cemetery is called 'The Home of Eternity'. What clues do these names give you about Jewish beliefs about death?

## Life is what matters

Whilst all Jews believe this life is not the only one, most do not spend their time and energy trying to work out exactly what will happen next. The author of Ecclesiastes wrote, 'There is no way for us to know what will happen after we die' (Ecclesiastes 3:22) and a great rabbi said, 'What can we know of death, we who cannot understand life?' (Reform Prayer Book).

Most Jews believe what matters most is getting on with this life. After all, they are convinced that what you do now will affect what happens next.

Funeral halls like the one shown in **A** are known by the Hebrew name Bet ha-Hayyim, which means 'The House of Life'. To stress the importance of life, friends and family who are mourning the loss of a loved one will be greeted at the funeral with the words, 'May you have a long life'.

> Some Jews think:
> Life = body and soul.
> Death = the separation of the body and the soul.
> **Resurrection** = body and soul.

# Two Jews, three opinions!

It is a standing joke in Judaism that when a group of Jews get together to discuss something, lots of different opinions emerge! What happens after a person dies is no exception.

> I believe that God will save the world in the future. He will bring peace and give us a spiritual leader called the **Messiah**. When that time comes, good people will be brought back to life to enjoy God's perfect world. For that reason, when I die I want my body buried, not destroyed by fire.

> I believe in resurrection but I don't think it is a one-off event. I think your soul can be reborn into the world several times. Yes, that's **reincarnation** and some Jews think that is what happens. For me, resurrection is an on-going process. The souls of righteous people return to mend the world.

**B**

> I believe in life after death but I don't think the body is resurrected. No, for me, life after death is a spiritual resurrection. I think we should interpret the ancient teachings in terms of today's world. I don't have any problems with cremation because I think the body is just a container for the soul.

Jews agree that death is not the end and believe God will judge people on what they did in this life. He will reward those who have led a good life by bringing their soul close to him. Those who have done wrong will be punished. Their soul will be sent to hell to be cleansed of its sin. Someone said it will be rather like putting dirty clothes in a washing machine. There is a lot of harsh churning of the washing, but it won't last forever. Eventually the object will come out clean. Only when the soul has been cleansed of its sins is it ready to enter God's presence.

Because God is merciful, Jews believe he will forgive those people who repent before they die and are genuinely sorry for their sins.

# How do I know it's true?

## The revelation of God's word

In early times, God revealed to people how they should behave. Some, like Adam and Noah, did their best to follow God's way but many did not.

Hundreds of years later, God revealed his instructions directly to the patriarchs. Abraham, the first and most important patriarch, was convinced there is only one God who should be worshipped. When God told Abraham to take his tribe on a 1,400 mile journey to set up a new homeland in Canaan (modern-day Israel), Abraham obeyed. God told him, 'I will give you many descendants, and they will become a great nation' (Genesis 12:2). Jews trace their descent from Abraham, his son Isaac and grandson Jacob.

God's revelation to humanity was completed many years later on Mount Sinai. Moses obeyed God and climbed the mountain while the people of Israel waited at the foot as they were told. In the middle of thunder and lightning, God proclaimed the Ten Commandments to the Jews. Orthodox Jews believe every Jewish soul that will ever exist was present at the foot of Mount Sinai and received the Torah from God. Moses told his followers, 'You are not the only ones with whom the Lord is making this Covenant with its obligations. He is making it with all of us who stand here in his presence today and also with our descendants who are not yet born' (Deuteronomy 29:14–15).
This means every Jew has been given the Torah by God. If God kept his part of the Covenant, then every Jew must keep theirs (see pages 8–9).

# The Orthodox Jewish view of truth

After God gave the Ten Commandments to the Jews, he revealed the rest of the Torah to Moses. Orthodox Jews believe that Moses wrote it down exactly as God told him, which is why the Torah is also called the Five Books of Moses. God went on to tell Moses many other things which Moses learned by heart and taught his followers by word of mouth. This is known as the **Oral Torah**. Later, these teachings were written in 63 volumes and the books are also known by their Hebrew name, the **Mishnah**. The Mishnah helps Jews to understand how to put the Torah into practice.

The revelation on Mount Sinai was the last time God handed down teachings to his people. The prophets who followed Moses were inspired by God to reinforce the Sinai teachings, but they never added anything new. Orthodox Jews believe it is possible for people today to have a personal experience of God, but God will never add to the Torah. The Torah contains everything that is necessary for life. People have to use their God-given intelligence to study the Torah and discover its meaning.

# The Liberal and Reform Jewish view of truth

Jewish scholars from both the Liberal and Reform traditions do not think the Torah contains the exact words dictated by God. This is because they have found evidence of at least four different styles of writing in the scriptures which has led them to date the Torah to several centuries after Moses.

This does not mean Liberal or Reform Jews disregard the Torah. They believe it is a valuable document containing teachings that will always have significance. Although they believe the Torah was written by humans, they are convinced the authors were inspired by God. For these Jews, the Torah contains God's message but, because it was written down by humans, it may contain human errors.

Liberal and Reform Jews are open to the possibility that God may inspire people in the future with information to help them live their lives the way God requires.

**Activity**

1 Orthodox Jews believe that many of the problems we face are the same today as they were 1,000 years ago. Write down *two* types of personal problems that you think are unchanged by history.

2 a As a class, brainstorm *four* problems that have been caused by modern technology. Areas to consider could be medical science, computers, etc.

  b Look at the Ten Commandments (Exodus 20) to see if there is anything there that could be adapted to answer the problems.

**Activity**

3 a Can you state *one* fact which you think is true now and will remain true forever?

  b Are there any facts which you think may not remain true forever?

4 Draw two columns on your page.

  a Head one column: 'Orthodox Truth'. Under this heading, write the advantages of having a fixed version of the law.

  b Head the other column: 'Liberal and Reform Truth'. Under this heading, write the advantages of having a flexible version of the truth that can be interpreted according to the time and the culture.

  c Which version would you prefer to live with? Why?

5 a Which group of Jews says the answer to everything you need to know is in the Torah?

  b Why would the other group(s) disagree?

# Scientific truth

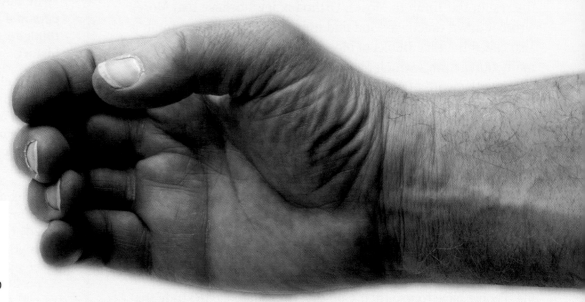

**A** One learned Jewish scholar said that science and religion were opposed to one another like the thumb and fingers are. They are not rivals, in fact they can work together to help us grasp things better.

## Are religion and science enemies?

Many Jews would say, 'No'. The two are more like partners. This is not a modern view either. The twelfth-century scholar and rabbi, Moses Maimonides, said that science can actually be a pathway to God. He argued that detailed scientific study of the natural world leads us to a better understanding of the amazing power of God.

Take the example of the human brain. The more scientists study how the brain works, the more amazed they are by its sheer complexity and power. Despite technological advances, we are a long way from understanding fully how a brain works. In fact, this has led some people to marvel at the brain's creator. For surely, they say, the brain is proof of the existence of God. Nothing as complex as a brain could happen by chance. There must have been an intelligent designer.

## Using science

Jews do not necessarily feel threatened by science. Instead, they see it as something God has given them and which they are free to use for the good of humanity. This is particularly true in the field of medicine. A leading rabbi said he was delighted by the advances in the understanding of DNA because it would lead scientists to discover treatments for various diseases. When critics have accused medical experts of 'playing God', the Chief Rabbi has disagreed saying, 'There is nothing sacrosanct [precious] about human suffering. What we can cure, we should.' He went on to quote a rabbi who said, 'We are God's partners in the work of creation.'

1 a Why do some people think religion and science are enemies?

b What might a Jew say to contradict this view?

**B** Professor Robert Winston is a leading British fertility doctor as well as a television personality. He helps couples who are having difficulties in conceiving a baby. As an Orthodox Jew, Professor Winston can see no problem in using the technological advances in medical science to help women become pregnant.

# Asking scientific questions

Some people mistakenly think religious people have to believe everything they are told without asking questions. Jews disagree. Asking questions, scientific or otherwise, is a healthy thing to do. It doesn't mean a person lacks faith, quite the opposite. The Chief Rabbi says asking questions about the universe and taking part in scientific investigation is actually a sign of faith. It shows the enquirer believes there are answers to be found.

Jews do not think the existence of the world was an accident. They believe it was deliberately created by God (see pages 6–7) and so there is meaning and purpose behind everything in nature.

As the highest point of creation, human beings were given a critical intelligence by God. Using this intelligence in the scientific study of God's creation is encouraged.

2 Role-play an interview between a scientist and an Orthodox Jew. What prejudices might the scientist have about the religious person?

3 a What did Moses Maimonides mean when he said scientific study could actually bring a person closer to God?

b How would someone argue the opposite case?

c What is your opinion?

4 What sort of ideas could religion help science to understand better? (Tip: You might wish to think about ethical issues, such as cloning animals.)

# Assessment for Unit 1

'The woman saw how beautiful the tree was and how good its fruit would be to eat, and she thought how wonderful it would be to become wise. So she took some of the fruit and ate it. Then she gave some to her husband, and he also ate it. As soon as they had eaten it, they were given understanding and realised that they were naked; so they sewed fig leaves together and covered themselves.

That evening they heard the Lord God walking in the garden, and they hid from him among the trees. But the Lord God called out to the man, "Where are you?" He answered, "I heard you in the garden; I was afraid and hid from you, because I was naked."

"Who told you that you were naked?" God asked. "Did you eat the fruit that I told you not to eat?"

The man answered, "The woman you put here with me gave me the fruit, and I ate it."'

(Genesis 3:6–12)

These questions test different sets of skills in RE. Which skills do you need to work on? Choose the level you need and work through the tasks set.

## Level 3

- What is the name that Jews give to the book that is quoted from here? Who wrote this book according to Orthodox Jews? Who was the author according to Liberal Jews?
- How would you describe Adam's reaction to God's questions? Give *two* examples from Adam's replies.
- How might you act if you were in a position similar to Adam's?

## Level 4

- Describe *three* sources of authority that Jews could turn to if they wanted to know what was right or wrong.
- Choose another religion and give *three* sources of authority a believer could turn to.
- What *three* sources of authority would you turn to if you wanted to know something? Explain which you value most, and why?

## Level 5

- Describe what Jews believe will happen after they die.
- How do the Orthodox and the Liberal Jewish differing views of life after death illustrate the different ways in which they see the value of Jewish sources?
- What is your view of life after death? How much has it been influenced by any particular religious or secular belief?

## Level 6

- Suggest *two* reasons why a scientist might say God does not exist. Suggest *two* reasons why another scientist would have no difficulty being Jewish?
- Professor Fred Hoyle said that the chances of a planet 'happening' to have the right conditions for human life were as likely as a hurricane passing through a scrapyard and creating a jumbo jet. What reasons could he give for the existence of life on earth? How convincing do you find his hurricane argument? What would you say are the reasons why we are here?

# Who is responsible?

We make choices at different stages of our lives and with these choices often come new freedoms and rights as well as new responsibilities.

- This is Rachel, a young Jewish woman who is clearly enjoying her wedding day. Find out what responsibilities she will now have to undertake as an Orthodox Jewish wife? What additional ones will she have when she becomes a mother?

- Choose *three* stages in your life. Write down the rights you might expect to gain at these ages. Then add the responsibilities they could bring.

# Your choice!

## glossary

Kippah
Kosher
Laws of Kashrut
Liberal Jew
Mitzvah
Mitzvot
Orthodox Jew
Reform Jew
Shabbat
Synagogue
Torah

*Why bother choosing to do things the Jewish way? Half the time no one would know if you did or you didn't!*

*Well, I'd know if I didn't do things properly. I'd feel I'd let myself down and more so if I went around pretending. You can't cheat God. He knows exactly what I am doing and thinking. Anyway, I am Jewish and proud of it. It's like if you are playing football, you don't pick up the ball and run into the goal with it! If you choose to play, then you play by the rules.*

**CHOCOLATE DREAM**

**Chocolate Dream combines thick plain chocolate with a crunchy biscuit**

Ingredients: Wheat flour, Plain chocolate (23%) (Sugar, Cocoa Mass, Cocoa Butter, Vegetable Fat, Anhydrous Milk Fat, Emulsifier: Soya Lecithin, Flavouring), Vegetable Oil, Wholemeal Flour, Sugar, Glucose Syrup, Invert Sugar Syrup, Raising Agents (Sodium Bicarbonate, Ammonium Bicarbonate), Salt, Wheat Bran.

Plain chocolate contains:
Cocoa Solids 41 per cent minimum.
Suitable for Vegetarians.

**A** A Jewish person will look at the labelling on food to check whether the product keeps the kosher dietary laws. K shows it is kosher. D shows it contains dairy products. LBD shows it has been checked by the London Bet Din.

## What shall I eat?

We all make decisions about what we are going to eat. It might involve what we like and don't like, or what is good and bad for our health. Jews also have to decide whether the food is **kosher**, in other words whether the **Torah** permits them to eat it.

The **Laws of Kashrut** appear in Leviticus 11 and elsewhere in the Torah, making them a **mitzvah**. Most Jews do not find it difficult to keep the rules and agree it actually makes for a healthy diet.

**B**

### The kosher dietary laws

- Meat must come from an animal that has cloven hooves and chews the cud.
- Fish must have fins and scales.
- Birds must be farmed.
- Animals must be killed with a single cut to the throat and the meat washed free of blood.
- Meat and milk must not be eaten together.

1 a What would the kosher label in **A** tell a Jew about the contents of this product?

b What other foods could you include with the chocolate biscuit to make a kosher packed lunch?

2 Of course it is possible for a Jew to cheat the kosher rules and secretly eat the wrong things. How do you think a Jew would feel? Who would know? Do you think it matters?

# What shall I wear?

We all face the daily decision of what to wear in the morning. Of course, there may be little choice if school uniform or special clothing for work is compulsory. **Liberal** and **Reform Jews** feel free to wear what they wish but **Orthodox** men regard the **kippah** as a compulsory religious garment. Orthodox men and women are expected to dress modestly and not flaunt their body with tight or revealing clothes. Married women cover their hair outside of the home. You might notice that the newly-married bride on page 25 has covered her hair.

> **Activity**
>
> 3 It is quite normal for young people to wear similar clothes to their particular friends. Why do they do this? Would it change the friendship if one member of the group decided to wear something totally different to the rest?
>
> 4 Compose an e-mail you could send to the boy in **C**. What would you like to ask him?

C For some Jews, religious clothing is a matter of choice. For others, it is a traditional requirement. This boy wears the religious clothing of an ultra-Orthodox Jew.

# How shall I spend the weekend?

From sunset Friday until nightfall Saturday is **Shabbat**, the day of the week the Torah commands is set aside for Jews to rest with their families. Today, these **mitzvot** are interpreted to forbid switching on electricity; travelling by car or public transport; going shopping; or attending places of entertainment. All house cleaning and hot food preparations must be finished before Shabbat begins so everyone can relax. Members of the family get home from school and work in time to welcome in Shabbat in the traditional way. Apart from attending **synagogue**, an Orthodox Jew takes the opportunity to study the Torah and enjoy time with their family and friends.

Reform Jews also value Shabbat as a day different to the rest of the week. It is a time for communal prayer, Torah study and family, but it is the values of Shabbat rather than the rules that matter most.

D Because I am Jewish my parents expect me to stay at home on Saturday afternoon when I want to go shopping with my friends. Why can't I do what I like? Does it matter if I tell them one thing and do something else? They won't find out.

*Naomi*

> **Activity**
>
> 5 Write an answer to letter **D** which appeared in a Jewish magazine. What will the editor tell Naomi to do and why?

# Is it right or is it wrong?

objective

to learn how the Torah is applied to problem solving

glossary

Rabbi
Ten
    Commandments

## Finding the answer

While most Jews believe the Torah contains everything they need to know in order to lead the life God requires, they can find it difficult to locate the exact solution to their problem. The scriptures, which were written thousands of years ago, don't always mention the dilemmas people are confronted with today. This is when it is necessary for a Jew to turn to a person in authority, a **rabbi**. He, or perhaps she in the Liberal or Reform traditions, looks beyond the specific problem to consider what principle is at stake. When that is established, then they look in the Torah to see where that principle was dealt with.

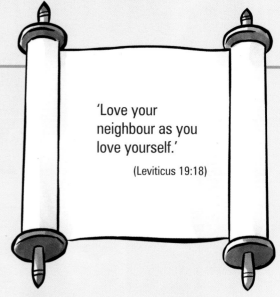

'Love your neighbour as you love yourself.'

(Leviticus 19:18)

**A** Some Jews have said this sums up everything you need to know when making decisions. Think of a situation where this might help a person come to the right solution.

**B**

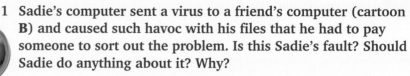

**Activity**

1 Sadie's computer sent a virus to a friend's computer (cartoon **B**) and caused such havoc with his files that he had to pay someone to sort out the problem. Is this Sadie's fault? Should Sadie do anything about it? Why?

2 Look at the **Ten Commandments** in Exodus 20 to see if any of them can be applied to the following cases:

a Jon has got a new state-of-the art camera-phone and Lisa is envious; she would really like one herself.

b Paula had a big row with her Mum after being wrongly accused of borrowing the car. Paula became abusive.

The quotation from Leviticus in **A** is hard to apply to Sadie's computer virus and the Torah certainly will not make reference to computer problems! The rabbi decided the following passage in Exodus dealt with the principle. Read it and see if you can make any connection between the two situations.

'If a bull gores someone to death, it is to be stoned, and its flesh shall not be eaten; but its owner is not to be punished. But if the bull had been in the habit of attacking people and its owner had been warned, but did not keep it penned up – then if it gores someone to death, it is to be stoned, and its owner is to be put to death also.'

(Exodus 21:28–29)

At first sight there seems to be no connection between a bull and a computer, but both cases involve a person owning something which causes damage. So the bull who kills someone = the computer that spreads a virus.

The bull suddenly turned nasty without warning and killed someone. Whilst the Torah thinks the animal should be disposed of immediately for everyone's safety, the owner is not to blame. He does not get off scot-free though. The rabbis judged that he should pay half damages which they calculated as half the value of the carcass.

In the second case, where the owner knew his bull was dangerous but never did anything about it, he is liable to pay full damages. Although the Torah says it is a life for a life, the rabbis decided only God could exact the death penalty and they fined him a large sum.

Apply the same concepts to the computer virus. Are viruses likely to happen to computers? If the answer is yes, what should a responsible computer owner do about it? If the owner does nothing and, as a result, passes a virus on, the Torah would hold them 100% liable.

What do you think Sadie should do about the situation?

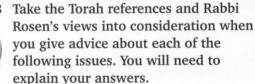 A young Jewish teenager is tempted to have a tattoo because their favourite footballer has got them. Is this allowed?

# Tattoos

Tattoos are a modern fashion statement but Rabbi Jeremy Rosen said the Torah actually discussed this issue thousands of years ago. There are several instances of people being told not to harm their bodies. Leviticus also says:

'Do not… tattoo yourselves or cut gashes in your body to mourn the dead.'

(Leviticus 19:27–28)

Writing in the *Jewish Telegraph*, the rabbi says:

I believe there is something holy in the body God has given us and although intervention to correct a defect or repair damage has its place, and so does cosmetic enhancement, the permanent use of our bodies as advertising hoarding strikes me as unholy.

(*Jewish Telegraph* 30 September 2005)

3  Take the Torah references and Rabbi Rosen's views into consideration when you give advice about each of the following issues. You will need to explain your answers.

- Can I have laser surgery to improve my short-sightedness?

- Can I have my ears pierced?

- Is some nip and tuck plastic surgery acceptable?

- Are recreational drugs permitted?

# Family life

Being a member of a family brings love and security. There is someone you can turn to when you have problems, be they emotional, financial or about health. In order for love and care to work in a family, everybody has to play their part. For someone to be able to receive help when they need it, they have to be prepared to give it when someone else needs it. Being a member of a family brings responsibilities which the Jewish scriptures offer rules and advice about.

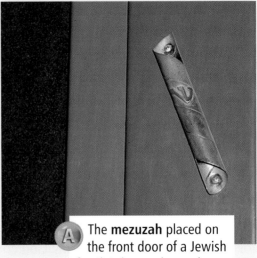

A  The **mezuzah** placed on the front door of a Jewish family's home shows that God has a place in the home. It also shows that family life plays an important part in Judaism.

## The responsibilities of children

'Respect your father and your mother, so that you may live a long time in the land that I am giving you.'

(Exodus 20:12)

'Make your father and mother proud of you; give your mother that happiness.'

(Proverbs 23:25)

'Listen to your father; without him you would not exist. When your mother is old, show her your appreciation.'

(Proverbs 23:22)

'See that they [elderly parents] eat and drink and take them where they need to go.'

(The Talmud)

1  Write a paragraph of practical advice for Jewish children based on the scriptural teachings opposite. Remember, the parent and child relationship still exists even if the child is 50 and their dad 75!

## The responsibilities of parents

'He who does not teach his son a trade is as though he taught him to be a robber.'

(The Talmud)

'Hear O Israel, the Lord our God is one God. Love the Lord your God with all your heart, with all your soul, and with all your strength. Never forget these commands that I am giving you today. Teach them to your children.'

(The Shema in Deuteronomy 4:6–7)

2  Either explain what the quotation from the Talmud opposite means or write a story to demonstrate the truth of the quotation.

3  Draw a poster showing how Jewish family life is a two-way responsibility.

# The Jewish mother

Some people regard their mother as central to their home and this is especially true for Jews. In Orthodox and Reform Judaism, the religion can only be passed on through the mother. This means you are Jewish if your mother is but you cannot inherit your Jewish birthright through your father. Liberal Jews accept a person as Jewish if either parent is a Jew.

A Jewish mother is responsible for teaching religious traditions to her children. This would include how to make sure food is kosher, the correct way to behave, preparations for Shabbat and festivals, as well stories from the religion. It is generally agreed that the way we have been brought up shapes the adult we become. This makes the importance of the mother in Judaism understandable.

 Family life is at the heart of Judaism. It is from the family a person gains their Jewishness.

# The Jewish father

A Jewish father has his duties too. They are different but equally important though many of them are outside of the home. It is a father's responsibility to provide for his family so that they have a home and food. He also takes responsibility for his children's behaviour until they come of age, which is aged 12 for a girl and 13 for a boy. A father must make sure his child has been taught the religion and that they practise it.

Jewish scriptures are clear that a father has a duty to ensure his son has practical skills. Look at the quotation from the **Talmud** about teaching the son a trade. One early rabbi also insisted that a father had a duty to teach his son to swim as an essential survival skill. What do you think is an essential survival skill today?

4 Design either a Parents' Charter or a Children's Charter. It should contain *five* things the family must do for them and *five* responsibilities they have towards others in the family.

5 Why do you think Orthodox Judaism will only accept a person as Jewish through their mother? (Tip: Look at the mother's job in the home.)

6 Do you think it would be helpful if everyone's duties and responsibilities in your family were clearly defined? Why?

C My Mum says that I should not stay out after 9 o'clock. I think that is stupid. I am not going to do anything at 9.15 that I wouldn't do at 8.30! Do I have to take any notice of her? It's my life and I've got a right to make up my own mind.

7 What advice would you give the person who wrote the letter in **C**? Is there any more information you would like to know before you decide on your response?

# Saying sorry

### objective

to understand the Jewish concept of repentance

### glossary

Free will
Prophet
Rosh Hashanah
Taslich
Teshuvah
Yom Kippur

If there is bad feeling in a family or between friends, it seems to hang in the air and everyone feels uncomfortable. Until the problem is sorted out, no one can move forward. It takes one person to say sorry for things to change, then everybody begins to feel better.

This is the idea behind **Teshuvah**, the Hebrew word for repentance. It involves saying sorry and asking the person you have hurt to forgive you. Jews believe God cannot forgive a person's sins until they have first asked the person they wronged for forgiveness.

**A** When something like this happens, you could 'cut the atmosphere with a knife'.

**B**

### Steps to Teshuvah

Step 1  Admit to yourself that you have done wrong and regret it.
Step 2  Find the person you hurt and ask their forgiveness.
Step 3  Then ask God's forgiveness for the wrong you did.
Step 4  Don't do it again!

**C** Many Jews symbolically wash away their sins at New Year. Little pieces of bread, or just crumbs and fluff from their pockets, are dropped into flowing water in the ceremony of **Taslich**. The **prophet** Micah said, God 'will trample our sins underfoot and send them to the bottom of the sea!'

## It takes two

Just as it takes two to have an argument, it takes two to heal one. Being truly sorry and asking for forgiveness is only one part; being prepared to accept someone's apology and put an end to grudges is as important.

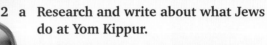

**D**

Chief Rabbi, Professor Jonathan Sacks, tells the story of two friends who had fallen out and not spoken to each other for 10 years. During the Ten Days of Repentance the rabbi goes over to each in turn and tells them that the holiest moment in the year is about to arrive. The time has come for them to apologise to one another and make up. 'Life,' he says, 'is too short to bear a grudge.' They agree, walk over to one another and shake hands. One says to the other, 'I wish you all that you wish me'. The second turns to the rabbi and says, 'You see – again he's starting with me!'

**Activity**

1  a  **What is the Chief Rabbi trying to teach people about saying sorry in the humorous story in D?**

   b  **How far up the steps of Teshuvah do you think the men in the story have come?**

> *Repent one day before you die.*
> (Rabbi Eliezer)

You might think this sounds fine because you can do what you like all the rest of the time and get away with it. Can you? What in fact Rabbi Eliezer was suggesting was that Jews continually repent because they never know when the end will come.

Jews believe that we all have **free will**. This means we can all choose to say we are sorry for things we have done wrong. If Rabbi Eliezer's words are taken to heart, Jews would do their best to apologise to people they have hurt as soon as possible. For all sorts of reasons, immediate apologies don't often come, but Judaism sets a time when quarrels should be settled.

## Wiping the slate clean

Making New Year's resolutions are not restricted to Jews. People often set out to improve themselves by perhaps resolving to give up smoking or take more exercise the following year. During the Ten Days of Repentance at Jewish New Year, Jews reflect on past mistakes and take the opportunity to make amends to the people they have wronged. On the last of the 10 days, **Yom Kippur**, they show God that they are truly sorry for all their sins and ask his forgiveness. This enables them to start the New Year afresh.

**Activity**

2  a  **Research and write about what Jews do at Yom Kippur.**

   b  **Explain what this has to do with forgiveness.**

3  **Reply to Josh's e-mail to the rabbi in E. When you advise Josh on what he should do, you will need to give your reasons.**

4  a  **What are the advantages in setting aside one day a year when everybody says sorry and makes a fresh start?**

   b  **What are the disadvantages?**

**E**

| Send Now | Send Later | | 〇〇〇 |
| --- | --- | --- | --- |

To: robert.smith1@religions&beliefs.rel.uk
Cc:
Attachments:

Toby took my girlfriend Shelley off me. We had a big row over her and haven't spoken since. Shelley's as bad. I told her so to her face. Frankly, I don't see why I should go out of my way to apologise to anyone but **Rosh Hashanah** is coming up. So what am I supposed to do about it?

*Josh*

33

# I'm responsible now

## objective

to learn about the religious responsibilities an adult Jew has

## glossary

Bar Mitzvah
Bat Chayil
Bimah
Minyan
Tallit
Tefillin

> Do you have any special religious responsibilities because you are a Jew?

> Well, I suppose I do, but I never think about it like that. It is just part of normal life, isn't it? We all have things we have to do. I've made a list of my special religious responsibilities.

## Sam's religious duties

Like all Jewish boys, I had my **Bar Mitzvah** (my coming-of-age ceremony) when I was 13. This means that from now on I am totally responsible for how I keep my religion. I can't blame it on my Dad now! Who will know if I shirk? Well, I will and so will God.

I have a duty to make up the **minyan** – that is one of the 10 adult males who need to be present for a synagogue service to take place. It is a big responsibility and it does make you feel grown up. Being able to be called up to the **bimah** for the reading of the Torah is another great honour.

I take my duty to pray three times a day seriously. In the morning, I put on my **tefillin** and **tallit** and say prayers along with my Dad, but when I've been away I have still prayed alone.

Friday night is synagogue attendance to welcome in Shabbat. If Dad's home, I walk down with him. Saturday? Well it is no different really. We always go to morning service as a family but, of course, I sit downstairs with the other men now. I did before my Bar Mitzvah most of the time, but as a child you can sit with your mother in the women's gallery if you want.

Now I have to keep the fast at Yom Kippur. This is the holiest day of the year when you go without food and drink for 25 hours. It's hard all right! But, because it is a real effort, you feel you are showing God that you are *truly* sorry for your sins of the previous year.

As a Jewish person I have to get married, but that's no hardship. I'd love to! I will feel that I am taking my part in the divine plan if I marry and have children. As an Orthodox Jew, I believe it is my religious responsibility to marry a Jewish girl to ensure my children are Jewish.

1 Role-play a radio phone-in with Sam. Write down *three* questions you would like to ask him about his responsibilities.

2 At the Bar Mitzvah ceremony the father says: 'Blessed is the One who has freed me from responsibility for the boy's sins.' Do you think a father should ever take responsibility for his child's behaviour? If so, up to what age? If not, who else is responsible?

# Esther's religious duties

I came of age at my **Bat Chayil** ceremony when I was 12 and I have kept the Yom Kippur fast strictly since then.

Like Sam, prayer is an important part of my religious life but women don't have the same fixed prayer times. This is sensible because if you have children demanding your attention, or food in the oven, you can't just drop everything to pray at that very moment.

Now I'm Bat Chayil, it is my responsibility to welcome in Shabbat if my mother is away. I am able to assist in keeping a kosher home.

As a Jew, it is my duty to marry and I want to marry another Jew. Because I take my responsibilities very seriously, I am going to ask the community for introductions to suitable Orthodox men. Marriage is too important to be left to a chance meeting with Mr Right!

I love the idea of being a Jewish mother and taking an important role in the religious upbringing of my children.

Yes, there are religious responsibilities for a Jewish girl. And, yes, some are different to Sam's, though I wouldn't say that makes me more important or less important. It's just different.

3 a Research the preparations for a Bar Mitzvah or a Bat Chayil ceremony. Then present your information in the form of a leaflet. Make sure you explain how the ceremony you have chosen prepares a young person for undertaking their religious responsibilities.

b Use a table to record the different religious responsibilities each person refers to.

4 Do you think having a big family party to celebrate your 18th birthday would help to make you aware of your new adult status? Why?

The words of the Rabbi Israel Salanter teach Jews how important it is to take personal responsibility.

When I was young, I wanted to change the world. I tried, but the world didn't change. So I decided to change my town, but my town didn't change. Then I resolved to change my family, but my family didn't change. Then I realised – first I have to change myself.

(Rabbi Israel Salanter)

35

# The student dilemma

**objective**

to look at the ways the Jewish community can help young people with their religious life

**glossary**

Anti-Semitism
Shiur
Yom Tov

**A**

I have really been looking forward to going to uni. Since I watched that series on hospital life on TV, I have wanted to be a surgeon. I worked hard for my GCSEs and A levels so I could get a place to study medicine. Now I am about to go, I am bothered about whether I will find student life a problem. I really want to make a go of it.

It will be the first time I have lived away from my home and I don't know anyone in the area. I'd like to share a house with other students but will they understand the importance of my religious life to me? I need some help really because I do want to get out and enjoy my student life before I settle down to the serious responsibilities of being a surgeon in a big hospital. But, at the same time, I do want to be true to myself and to my faith.
Help!

Simon

1 Describe the sort of problems you think Simon in **A** might encounter at university as an Orthodox Jew.

GIVING STRENGTH TO **ALL** JEWISH STUDENTS

**B** The Jewish Chaplaincy says: 'Jewish students, most of them living away from home, are facing ever greater threats on campus. From anti-Semitism and intermarriage to drugs and missionary activity, the list of problems is a daunting one. That's why our chaplains are there for every Jewish student for every possible reason.'

2 List the problems the Jewish Chaplaincy says Jewish students face today. Explain why these might cause greater problems for Jews than other students.

# Hillel House

Twenty-two universities in the UK have a special hall of residence that provides Jewish accommodation on their campus, it is called Hillel House. Here, students can choose to live with other Jewish students and attend events that have a particular Jewish flavour. Some Hillel Houses are self-catering so students are free to eat as they want; others provide kosher meals.

The Jewish Chaplaincy is a modern organisation that is there to support each Jewish student.

Read what they offer:

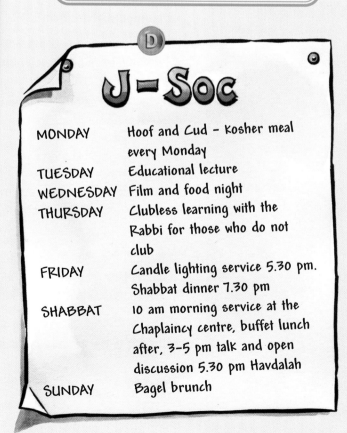

C The Union of Jewish Students with the Chief Rabbi as a guest.

'The chaplains and their families instil a warmth and love to individual students both in their own homes and in events organised under the auspices of the local Hillel Houses and Jewish Societies.

The chaplain's role encompasses not only religious and pastoral duties, both on and off campus, but also 24-hour work including counselling for bereavement, stress, drugs and loneliness. It is not uncommon for the chaplain's home to be a hive of activity well into the night as students gather for a **shiur** or a chocolate fondue evening, for a quiet chat or to prepare for the upcoming **Yom Tov** or Shabbat meals.

The chaplaincy service is vital for each and every Jewish student on UK campuses. With the rise of extremism, **anti-Semitism**, missionary activities and fundamental groups against Jews, the chaplain's role is becoming even more vital.'

**Activity**

3 Write Simon an e-mail replying to his concerns and offering advice based on the information you have read about on these pages. Do you think Simon was right to be concerned, or has he over-reacted?

D

## J-Soc

| | |
|---|---|
| MONDAY | Hoof and Cud – Kosher meal every Monday |
| TUESDAY | Educational lecture |
| WEDNESDAY | Film and food night |
| THURSDAY | Clubless learning with the Rabbi for those who do not club |
| FRIDAY | Candle lighting service 5.30 pm. Shabbat dinner 7.30 pm |
| SHABBAT | 10 am morning service at the Chaplaincy centre, buffet lunch after, 3–5 pm talk and open discussion 5.30 pm Havdalah |
| SUNDAY | Bagel brunch |

What Simon has not had time to find out yet is that most universities have a J-Soc, that is a Jewish society that will give him all the assistance he needs and provide him with a good social life. He will also be able to join the Union of Jewish Students who work closely with J-Soc. Not only can he have a good time, but he will be able to continue developing his Jewish education and extend his circle of Jewish friends.

# Being a responsible citizen

Jews do not see any conflict in being Jewish and in being British, African, French or any other nationality. Their religion and their allegiance to the country they live in can exist side-by-side. It is no more of a problem than being dark-haired and tall.

The history of the Jewish people is full of examples of them being forced out of their land or taken prisoner and deported. As a result, they have learned to settle where they have found themselves and the scriptures have given guidance on how they should behave. As you will see, it is their requirement to work for justice that leads Jews to play their part as responsible citizens in their community.

From a young age, Jewish children in Israel are used to working together with all nationalities.

'Build houses and settle down. Plant gardens and eat what you grow in them. Marry and have children. Then let your children get married, so that they also have children. …Work for the good of the cities where I have made you go as prisoners. Pray to me on their behalf, because if they are prosperous, you will be prosperous too.'

(Jeremiah 29:5–7)

This extract above is from a letter written by the prophet Jeremiah to the Jews who had been taken prisoner and moved to Babylonia. Jews interpret this to mean that God wants them to support the country they live in.

'Do not ill-treat foreigners who are living in your land. Treat them as you would a fellow-Israelite, and love them as you love yourselves. Remember that you were once foreigners in the land of Egypt.'

(Leviticus 19:33–34)

'The law of the country is the law.'

(The Talmud)

'Work for peace within your household, then in your street, then in your town.'

(The Talmud)

'Pray for the welfare of the government; if it were not for the fear of it, men would swallow each other alive.'

(Ethics of the Fathers)

Greville Janner is a Jew who tries to put the Torah teachings about justice into practice in public life. He trained and worked as a lawyer, then in 1970 was elected Labour MP for Leicester, representing the needs of all his constituents (only a very small number of whom were Jewish) for 27 years. In 1997 he was honoured with a peerage, becoming a member of the House of Lords where, as Lord Janner of Braunstone, he continues to serve his country.

He has worked on committees concerned with human rights, employment law, consumer protection and the Commonwealth. Today, Lord Janner continues to campaign for anti-smoking legislation and road safety.

Not only has Lord Janner devoted his life to serving the British community, he has also assisted Jewish communities. When he joined the army at the age of 18, he served as the youngest War Crimes Investigator working at weekends with survivors from the Bergen Belsen concentration camp. His experiences with Holocaust survivors led him to create and build the **Holocaust** Educational Trust of which he remains the Chairman. This Trust aims to raise everyone's awareness and understanding of the Holocaust and to show its relevance today. This work has not been restricted to Britain because Lord Janner has taken an active interest in the Trust's work to locate and mark the Holocaust mass graves in the Baltic States. He has also been a key figure on the international scene in the fight to get compensation for victims of the Holocaust.

Lord Janner has devoted an important part of his life to assisting overseas communities. He has worked closely with leaders of other religions to build understanding and friendships. Together with Prince Hassan bin Talal of Jordan, Lord Janner is setting up an organisation which brings together Muslim and Jewish political leaders in the fight against **Islamaphobia** and anti-Semitism worldwide.

B  Lord Janner of Braunstone – a Jewish man who has served the British community for more than 50 years.

Activity

1  What part of Lord Janner's work do you consider to be the most valuable? Why?

2  Research the work of the Holocaust Educational Trust and prepare a brief presentation on its work. Explain why they believe it is important to remember the Holocaust.

C  Lord Janner addresses The Holocaust Education Trust.

# Getting involved

For some Jews, their faith means they feel an obligation to take an active part in the life of their community. It might be in their school, their town or at a national level.

**objective**

to look at examples of how Jewish people take responsibility for others in their community

**A**

Rafi Cohen is 17 and attends a non-Jewish school in Manchester. He said, 'I really want to make a difference to other pupils at the school.' This led him to accept a position of responsibility in his school as vice-captain. His concern about others' welfare in school led him to get involved in a peer-support scheme. He, along with others, trained in his spare time to become someone other pupils could talk to in confidence about their personal problems and be sure of getting the help they needed.

**B**

Naomi Tomlinson thinks it is important to get help to improve your school community. At her non-Jewish secondary school she wanted to do something practical to help her fellow pupils. 'I like the responsibility,' she said. 'If there is something I want to change about the school I can talk to the head teacher. There were no bag racks outside the library and we needed them. We spoke to teachers and now there is somewhere to put our bags. It sounds boring, but it's important to pupils' everyday lives.' Out of school, Naomi takes her religious responsibilities seriously and teaches the five to seven-year-old class at her local synagogue.

(*Jewish Telegraph* 23 September 2005)

1 Write a 150-word article for a newspaper explaining why a Jewish man or woman should consider joining the police force. Explain what they could contribute and why it is helpful to have practising Jews in the force.

2 Write a brief report to the Chief Constable explaining what things the force should be aware of when recruiting an Orthodox Jew. Points you might include would be diet; Shabbat observance; festivals; religious dress; and prayer times.

## Taking national responsibility

Dr Edie Friedman is an American Jew who came to Britain in the 1970s and has worked to involve the Jewish community in human rights issues. As a result of her work, the Jewish Council for Racial Equality (JCORE) was set up in 1976.

**Fighting crime, protecting people**

**Reflect the tradition: in and out of uniform.**

**JPA**

**Train to be a Police Officer**
Starting salary £18,264

Greater Manchester is a thriving and vibrant region, with some of the most diverse communities to be found anywhere in the UK and the largest provincial police force, with around 8,000 officers. All our Divisions have been structured to provide visible, local policing and, for some time now, we have been putting officers back into the heart of communities in response to community concerns.

At GMP, we're totally committed to reflecting the population we serve, although in some instances we haven't quite achieved that goal. Our Jewish population is the country's largest outside London and still growing, at around 30,000, with its own active and successful religious and cultural community. So we'd like an even higher representation of the Jewish community within our ranks.

As a police officer, you'll find the only predictability is unpredictability. So expecting the unexpected whilst motivating yourself to handle the routine, as well as the exciting occurrences that come along, will be your prime objectives.

Then of course there's the great satisfaction you'll get from a sense of contributing to society by maintaining law and order that makes this one of the great careers for men and women from any background, who are aged at least 18?

When you join us, you'll get comprehensive basic training to help you become a uniformed officer and ongoing support to help you progress. After two years there's a wide range of options to choose from – too many to list here – but few other careers can offer the same challenges.

And when you're out of uniform – either in a non-uniformed role or just off duty - there are standards to uphold because, as we've said, you're there to represent your community. If you believe you can meet our standards, then opt for a great career. As well as an excellent starting salary, the other benefits include health care and free travel on local transport.

**If you are fit, healthy and of good character, call our Positive Action Team on 0161 856 1141.**

**Greater Manchester POLICE**

www.gmp-recruitment.co.uk

**JCORE says:**
'As Jews, we know the consequences of racism only too well. For Black, Asian and other minority ethnic communities in Britain, discrimination, harassment and violent attacks remain an everyday occurrence.
We know what happens when others stand by and do nothing. That's why our community needs to speak out – to help to bring about change and challenge racism at its roots.'

3 a Dr Friedman said that her aim when setting up JCORE was for Jews to see 'the work of building a more economically and socially just society as part and parcel of what it means to be Jewish'. What does Dr Friedman mean by 'more economically and socially just'?

b Why would this involve working with Black and Asian groups and helping asylum seekers?

4 If you walked past a toddlers' playground and saw a little girl wandering off on her own, would you do anything? Why?

JCORE's projects include:

- race equality education with training courses and publications produced for schools and youth groups
- exhibitions to show the connections between Britain's Asian, Black and Jewish communities
- campaigning for rights for asylum seekers; help for children who arrive unaccompanied in Britain and projects to help refuge doctors re-qualify.

# Assessment for Unit 2

'Long ago, in the days before Israel had a king, there was a famine in the land. So a man named Elimelech… who lived in Bethlehem in Judah, went with his wife Naomi and their two sons Mahlon and Chilion to live for a while in the country of Moab… Elimelech died and Naomi was left alone with her two sons, who married Moabite women, Orpah and Ruth. About ten years later Mahlon and Chilion also died…

Some time later Naomi heard that the Lord had blessed his people by giving them a good harvest; so she got ready to leave Moab with her daughters-in-law. They started out together to go back to Judah, but on the way she said to them, "Go back home and stay with your mothers. May the Lord be as good to you as you have been to me and to those who have died… You must go back, my daughters… Why do you want to come with me? Do you think I could have sons again for you to marry?…" They started crying. Then Orpah kissed her mother-in-law goodbye and went back home, but Ruth held on to her [Naomi]… Ruth answered, "Don't ask me to leave you! Let me go with you. Wherever you go, I will go; wherever you live, I will live. Your people will be my people, and your God will be my God. Wherever you die, I will die, and that is where I will be buried…" When Naomi saw that Ruth was determined to go with her, she said nothing more.'

(Ruth 1:1–18).

These questions test different sets of skills in RE. Which skills do you need to work on? Choose the level you need and work through the tasks set

## Level 3

- Give *two* examples of how Ruth shows that she is responsible for her mother-in-law.
- What would a Jewish person say if you asked why it was important to look after the old, the young and the sick?
- How far can one person or family put into practice Jewish ideas of charitable activity?

## Level 4

- Give *three* examples of how Ruth's attitude towards Naomi might inspire people to behave today.
- Explain why it is important for Jewish people to have a religious marriage ceremony rather than a civil one. What sort of responsibilities are they choosing to undertake in a Jewish ceremony?
- Describe a situation when you chose to do something for someone else and got nothing out of it. What made you do it?

## Level 5

- Explain why some Jewish people believe they should take responsibility for the welfare of people they have never met.
- Ruth's behaviour was following in the footsteps of Abraham and the angels (Genesis 18:1–8) and Rebecca (Genesis 24:17–20). How do modern Jews try to copy this?
- Why do you think Jews get involved in fighting human rights abuse? Do you think it matters very much if it happens in a far away country or even if it happens here? Explain your reasons?

## Level 6

- Explain why some Jews feel it is their duty to speak out against injustice. Do you think it achieves anything worthwhile if the person ends up getting murdered?
- Compare the way a Jewish person makes decisions about right and wrong actions with a non-religious person. What sorts of things guide your decisions about right and wrong actions?
- Ruth was a Moabite, not a member of the Jewish people. Yet, she became the great grandmother of King David who was one of the greatest ever Jews. What do you think the author of the book of Ruth is teaching us?

# We're not on our own!

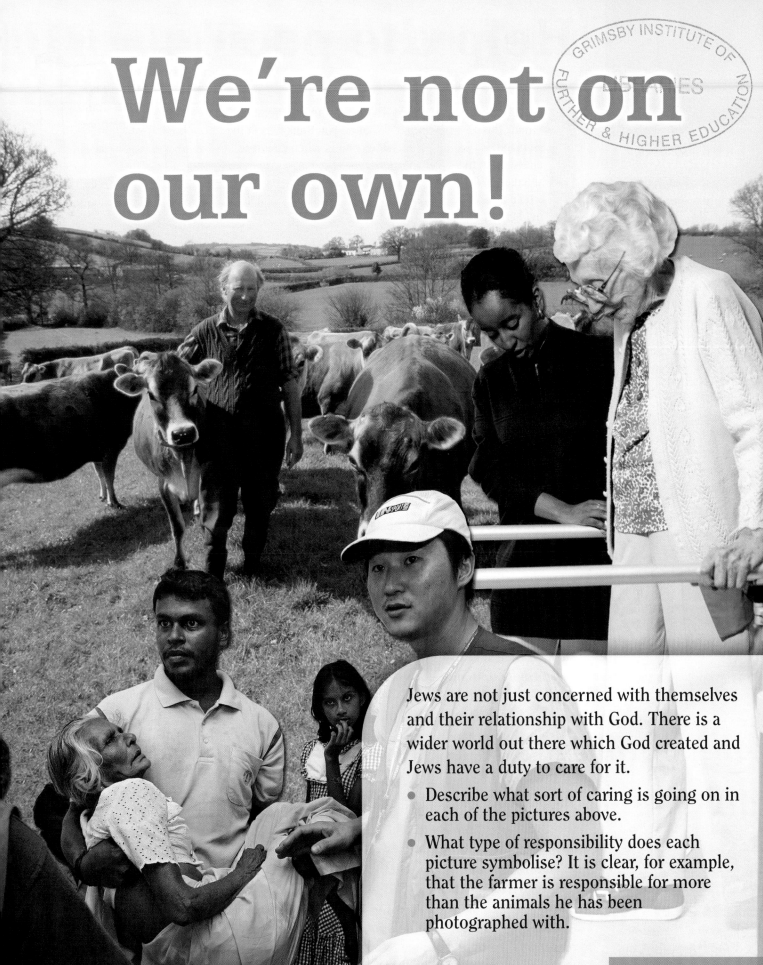

Jews are not just concerned with themselves and their relationship with God. There is a wider world out there which God created and Jews have a duty to care for it.

- Describe what sort of caring is going on in each of the pictures above.

- What type of responsibility does each picture symbolise? It is clear, for example, that the farmer is responsible for more than the animals he has been photographed with.

43

# Help the poor!

'Poverty is worse than fifty plagues.'
(The Talmud)

**objective**

to understand the Jewish approach to poverty

**glossary**

Fallow
Kippah
Moses Maimonides
Torah
Tzedakah
Tzedek

**A** How do you think this woman has ended up in this situation? What would it take to get her out of it?

**B** This seems an exaggerated claim. What do you think was in the writer's mind when he wrote this?

Every society has members who are poor and the **Torah** recognised this:

'There will always be some Israelites who are poor and in need, and so I command you to be generous to them.'

(Deuteronomy 15:11)

Once someone falls a long way behind the rest, it is very hard for them to get back on their feet. Lack of money leads to lack of food, to illness, to an inability to work to earn money, and so it goes on. It is a downward spiral. For some, possibly the woman in picture **A**, it is impossible to get out of the situation without help.

This is why the Torah contains many practical rules about how the poor should be helped. There are laws about gathering the harvest that tell the farmer to leave a small amount of his crop in the fields for the poor to gather (Deuteronomy 24:19–21). In another place, people are told to give a tenth of their crop to the poor every third year

(Deuteronomy 26:12) and to leave their fields **fallow** every seventh year. Not only does this rest the land but it gives the poor the chance to gather whatever grows. These are very practical ways in which the early Jews tried to prevent the poor from starving. Most British Jews are not farmers but they are still required to give a tenth of their income to the poor.

**C** **Tzedakah** means charity, helping the needy.
**Tzedek** means justice.

The two Hebrew words in **C** are closely connected because the ideas are linked. Judaism says charity is not about choosing whether or not to give a person some money. It is simply about justice. This is because it is only fair for people who have got money to give some to those who haven't. We are all human beings and we were all created by God.

**Global issues: poverty**

44

The following passage suggests another reason why rich people should share their wealth.

'So then, you must never think that you have made yourselves wealthy by your own power and strength. Remember that it is the Lord your God who gives you the power to become rich. He does this because he is still faithful today to the covenant that he made with your ancestors.'

(Deuteronomy 8:17–18)

1 'At the end of every seventh year you are to cancel the debts of those who owe you money.' (Deuteronomy 15:1) This rule was designed to prevent people becoming trapped in poverty. What would be the advantages and disadvantages of this law?

2 Write the script for a slot on a Jewish local radio programme. Explain why Jews should help the needy.

## Dignity

One of the worst things about having to accept charity is that it takes away a person's self-respect. No one likes asking for help, especially when it involves money. It is so embarrassing to have to hold out your hand to receive money from someone you have had to ask. People who have got the money to give can also feel awkward. The Jewish scholar, **Moses Maimonides**, knew this and he devised a table of eight degrees of charity beginning at the lowest level (**D**).

3 Draw *eight* cartoons, or write *eight* paragraphs, to give examples of how Moses Maimonides' eight degrees of charity could operate today.

4 Write a letter from Moses Maimonides to a Jewish factory owner asking for a charitable donation.

5 a What would a Jew say to someone who said, 'It is my money because I earned it!'?

b Do you think that you have a right to do what you like with money you have earned? Why?

c Would giving to charity be different if you had been left the money by a rich uncle?

---

**D**

### Eight degrees of charity

Level 1 Giving money grudgingly.

Level 2 Giving less than you can afford but kindly.

Level 3 Giving only because someone has asked you.

Level 4 Giving to a poor person before they ask.

Level 5 Giving money to a poor person who does not know you.

Level 6 Giving so the poor person does not know the giver.

Level 7 Giving in a completely anonymous way, so the giver does not know who will receive the money and the recipient doesn't know who donated.

Level 8 Helping set a person up in a job so they will never be dependent on charity again.

But remember that any charity given is better than none!

**E** If a Jewish man bought this **kippah**, which level on Moses Maimonides' scale would he achieve? Explain why.

# Helping the Jewish community

## objective

to look at ways in which a Jewish community puts tzedakah into practice

## glossary

Gemach
Kosher
Liberal Jew
Matzah
Orthodox Jew
Pesach
Pushke
Reform Jew
Shabbat
Synagogue
Yeshiva

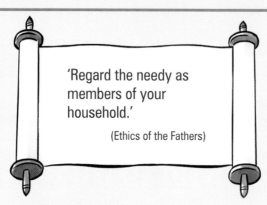

'Regard the needy as members of your household.'

(Ethics of the Fathers)

## Are there any poor and needy Jews in Britain today?

People often assume that everybody in society is getting richer but, sadly, this is not the case. More people are living into old age and some have very small pensions which mean they struggle to afford basic food, housing and warmth.

In the Jewish communities there can be poverty because **Orthodox Jewish** men sometimes choose to study the Torah full-time. This means they require financial assistance for themselves during their **yeshiva** studies. Many also have families that need supporting because Orthodox Jews are encouraged to marry young and have lots of children. Even those not studying at yeshiva can find it difficult to support a big family on one income.

Amongst the **Liberal** and **Reform Jews**, the causes of poverty may be different. Changes in the structure of society have led to more single-parent families who also find it hard to cope financially.

Can you think of anything else that might cause poverty?

## Charity begins at home

This is a favourite saying and one that is often used as an excuse for not giving money to worthy causes. In Judaism, charity does *begin* at home because children are taught how important charity is, but it should not end at home! It is customary for a Jewish family to have a charity box, known as a **pushke**, in the home into which family members drop bits of change. Children may well be encouraged to donate a little bit of their pocket money at times.

> **Activity**
>
> 1 Jews are taught that women come before men and relatives before strangers in the distribution of charity. Do you think there is any good reason for this rule?

**A** There are always charity collections in the synagogue. This is one of several in a Liberal synagogue and people are asked to drop in foreign coins left over from their holidays. This money will be converted into sterling and used to support an educational charity.

CHANGE FOR THE BETTER

WE WANT YOUR MONEY
What do you do with your foreign money after your holiday or business trip?
HOW ABOUT DOING SOME GOOD?
Let us change your foreign currency for Sterling and use the proceeds to fund ULPS Educational Projects.
Just put the currency into an envelope and return it to your synagogue or to the Montagu Centre.
WE WILL DO THE REST!

Global issues: poverty

46

# Community responsibility

It is quite common for a **synagogue** to have special collections. On a Thursday, the money is used to help the needy pay for **Shabbat** and at festival time special collections enable the poor to enjoy the celebrations as well. Donations of food as well as money are collected at the synagogue ahead of the festival of Purim, and before **Pesach** there is a special collection of 'wheat money'. It was originally given to the poor so they could buy the special flour to make the **matzah** – actually it was to buy potato flour, a substitute for wheat flour! Why?

Some members of the Jewish community take turns working in a cost shop. This gets its name because local Jewish grocers, bakers and butchers sell their produce to the shop at cost price, without making any profit. Because the shop is staffed by volunteers, the food can be sold to needy Jews in the community at the same price, which is much cheaper than they would pay elsewhere.

Jewish charities also care for the elderly and other vulnerable Jews. There are special homes that offer a permanent home to the elderly, as well as short-term care so family members can have a holiday. Other Jewish organisations offer special care for the disabled, the blind, mentally ill and those with drug and alcohol problems. Although these organisations may receive grants from the local authority, they are also supported by collections in the synagogue and locality.

**Gemachs** are lending organisations in the Jewish community. They arrange for people to borrow things they may need only for a short time and do not want to buy. This might range from a wheelchair to a wedding dress. In return, the borrower gives a small donation.

**Activity**

2  Study the different charitable activities that appear on these pages and decide which level each reaches on Moses Maimonides' scale (see pages 44–45).

3  Design a small poster that could go on a charity box to collect food donations in a local **kosher** supermarket.

4  What would you say to someone who thought wearing borrowed clothes on your wedding day was terrible?

TO SOME THIS IS BUT A DREAM!

JCD
Jewish Child's Day

Jewish Child's Day provides the essent and items that help to fulfil a suffering dreams…
Food, Clothing, Emergency Life Saving Medical Equipment, Wheelchairs, Therapy, Pets, Holidays, Toys, Books, Social and Educational Activities, Sports Equipment.

Please help Jewish Child's Day make some dreams come true for Jewish children in Britain, Israel, Eastern Europe, North Africa, wherever they are…

JCD
Jewish Child's Day

www.jewishchildsday.co.uk                    …dreams really can come true - with YOUR help

**B** This charity helps Jewish children around the world. Use their website to find out more about their activities and design a leaflet they could use to ask for donations.

# Jewish concern around the world

to examine case studies of Jewish humanitarian aid in the world

**A** Tzedek works with some of the poorest communities in the world, regardless of religion or race. What is their logo based on? Why is it an appropriate symbol for a Jewish charity?

## Case study 1

Tzedek has organised self-help groups in West Bengal, India. A successful one involved mushroom production. Until Tzedek came along, the men found it difficult to get work for more than half of the year. This made it hard for them to feed their families and young children had to be sent out to work as well. Tzedek trained men to grow mushrooms and to sell them at market. Families were loaned 3,000 rupees to buy seeds and equipment. Mushrooms were chosen because they could be grown near home, enabling the family to carry on with their original work as they built their business up. Not only would mushrooms earn the family money, but they also provided them with nutritious food. When the produce sold at the local market, the families were usually able to earn around 1,500 rupees a month.

(Based on Tzedek's website)

1 Why would Tzedek choose to work on a self-help project as part of their humanitarian aid? Look back to Moses Maimonides' advice on pages 44–45.

Activity

# Case study 2

One of World Jewish Relief's many projects has been based in Zaparozhye in Ukraine. Here, they have provided money to purchase and renovate a building to house a welfare centre and a Jewish community centre. The welfare centre is designed to look after the needs of the most vulnerable members of society, the very old and the very young. It has medical facilities; distributes food parcels; provides a day centre for the elderly; supports mothers with young children; and arranges home care for thousands of other needy people. The community centre, which has a school, nursery and children's home attached to it, holds events that will support the Jewish community in Zaparozhye. These range from cultural events to keep-fit sessions in the gym.

(Based on World Jewish Relief's website)

# Case study 3

Leonora Weil volunteered to help in Kenya. Here is part of her story.

> This summer, I joined the Jewish organisation Tzedek with 12 other students to volunteer in Nairobi, Kenya. I worked with two other British volunteers in Dagoretti Children's Centre. Dagoretti is a school and home for approximately 250 orphans, over 50% with AIDS, which is run through the auspices of 'Feed the Children'. The children I worked with were both mentally and physically handicapped as well as able-bodied...
> Everything is produced on site from the food and the clothes to the wheelchairs and furniture. The atmosphere is one of community and this is borne out by the children themselves: the able-bodied or the partially-disabled assisting those who require it. On site is also a workshop where disabled adults make jewellery and screen prints for sale.

Part of Leonora's job involved planning a two-week camp for the children that included arts and crafts as well as sports. She recalls the way the children coped.

> The determination of the children to overcome their difficulties was extremely inspiring. Children with no arms painted with their feet or teeth. One child who had no legs ran away from me in a game of tag using his arms and his waist... As well as variation due to the handicapped nature of the children, the cultural differences were apparent as well. Games like 'pass the parcel' are a totally different experience to children who may never have received a present before.

**2** Write an article for a Jewish newspaper about the World Jewish Relief's new welfare centre in Zaparozhye. Explain what it offers and the religious reasons behind its set-up. The teachings on pages 44–45 might help you.

**3** What everyday religious problems do you think an Orthodox Jew might face if they volunteered to work in Kenya as Leonora did? (Tip: Think about diet, etc.)

**4** Choose *one* of the case studies on these pages and plan a television publicity campaign. Your aim is to raise awareness of the problems and attract donations.

# What do Jewish teachings say about the environment?

ective

alyse Jewish
ings about the
onment

ssary

ardship

**A** Because the Torah opens with people in the middle of God's beautiful creation, Judaism shows special concern for the environment.

## What does the Torah say?

'Then the Lord God placed the man in the Garden of Eden to cultivate it and guard it.'

(Genesis 2:15)

'Your land must not be sold on a permanent basis, because you do not own it; it belongs to God, and you are like foreigners who are allowed to make use of it.'

(Leviticus 25:23)

'Then God said, "And now we will make human beings; they will be like us and resemble us. They will have power over the fish, the birds, and all animals, domestic and wild, large and small... Have many children, so that your descendants will live all over the earth and bring it under their control. I am putting you in charge of the fish, the birds, and all the wild animals."'

(Genesis 1:26 and 28)

**B**

The Torah teaches Jews that God has loaned them the earth to use. The natural world is given to them on trust and, although they can take what they need, they have a duty to care for it and return it in a good condition when they leave. The idea of caring for the planet and handing it on safely to the next generation is called **stewardship**.

1 List *three* things that Jews are told to do, or not to do, in the Torah passages in **B**. Compare your answers with a partner's and add any points you missed.

2 What does Leviticus 25:23 mean when it says people do not own land?

3 What practical problems could arise if we take what we need from the planet, yet have to pass it on in a good condition to the next generation?

issues:
nment

**C** This land was fought over in the First World War. The land was totally destroyed and did not grow anything for a long time. Such treatment of the earth is totally against Jewish teachings.

'When you are trying to capture a city, do not cut down its fruit trees, even though the siege lasts a long time. Eat the fruit, but do not destroy the trees; the trees are not your enemies.'

(Deuteronomy 20:19)

In fact, this quotation from Deuteronomy is taken to mean God forbids all wasteful destruction of the planet. This would mean dumping waste chemicals in the sea is forbidden because it could harm marine life.

The scriptures also require both animals and land to be rested. It is not just that both will work better if they have a break, but because it is fair. God rested on the seventh day after the creation of the world and so should humans. Although Jews are told to rest on Shabbat and let their animals rest, they must not neglect them. The Torah requires a person to feed their animals first before they rest on Shabbat. Even the land must rest. The Torah tells Jews to sow a field for six years then leave it fallow on the seventh. Any crops that grow in that field when it is fallow can be collected by the poor. What is left will be eaten by the wildlife.

**D**

One day as Honi, a very saintly man, was walking on the road he saw a man planting a fruit tree. 'How long does it take for that tree to bear fruit?' he asked him. The man said it would be 70 years. Honi asked, 'Are you sure you will live long enough to eat that fruit?' The man answered, 'I found fruit trees in the world because my ancestors planted them for me. So I am planting these for my children.'

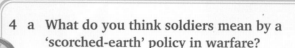

Activity

4 a What do you think soldiers mean by a 'scorched-earth' policy in warfare?

b Why would an army do this?

c What is the problem with this policy? Do you think it is ever justified?

5 Do you think the method of farming recommended in the Torah is old fashioned or ahead of its time? Why?

6 What would you say to someone who said, 'It's my life, no one else's. I shouldn't have to worry about the planet'?

7 'We are all passengers together in this fragile and glorious world.' This is part of a twentieth-century Jewish declaration on the environment. Use magazine photos or your own artwork to make a poster displaying this quotation. See if you can work in some biblical quotes as well.

8 How could a twenty-first-century Jew put the idea behind the ancient story and cartoon in **D** into practice today?

# Going green!

**A** This green construction is a sukkah. Families traditionally build their own temporary structure like this in the garden and hope to take their festive meals in it. In Britain this can sometimes be a chilly and damp experience!

### objective

to examine the ways Jews put teachings about the environment into practice

### glossary

Mitzvot
Noahide Laws
Shochet
Sukkah
Sukkot

The festival of **Sukkot** is a time when Jews remember how God looked after them as they wandered in the desert for 40 years. It is also a harvest festival that celebrates God's continuing care for his people in providing them with food. Jews build a temporary shelter, called a **sukkah** outside. It must have a roof of natural plants with space through to see the stars. The walls and ceiling are often decorated with fruits and other symbols of the harvest. For the week of the festival, meals are eaten there. The fragile nature of the sukkah reminds Jews of their dependence on God.

## Concern for animals

Jews are commanded to show respect and care for animals because they are part of God's creation. The **Noahide Laws** (see pages 8–9) lay down seven basic rules for any society. Number six is: 'Do not be cruel to animals'. This does not mean that animals can't be eaten. They can and the Torah gives clear guidance about the types of animals that are kosher. The Torah also sets out specific instructions about the way an animal must be killed in order to minimise its suffering. Only a trained Jewish slaughterer (a **shochet**) can kill an animal. It must be carried out without pre-stunning, but using a razor-sharp knife to slit the animal's throat.

There are also other **mitzvot** about animal welfare which state that an animal must not be killed within sight or sound of another. Hunting is not permitted as a sport nor for food because it prolongs an animal's suffering. Neither is it permitted to trap an animal for its fur.

**Activity**

1 a  Research the festival of Sukkot. Find out exactly how a sukkah is made.

b  What is a lulav and an etrog? What do they symbolise?

Global issues: environment

Although animals must be cared for, they are not equal to humans in God's world. In Genesis 1:28 God told Adam, 'I am putting you in charge of the fish, the birds, and all the wild animals.' This means that animals can be used to help humans and the Torah is clear that a person's life is of more value than an animal's. This means that most Jews would think that using animals for medical experiments is acceptable.

**B** There is no problem with Jews keeping pets. Here is Sooty, Sarah's much-loved cat.

**D** Sooty is always fed first in our house. This is because it says in the Torah animals should be fed before humans. She eats food that is kosher. To make it easier, Mum decided from the outset that Sooty would have fish cat food. It also means she can have milk if she wants, though she doesn't like it much. At Pesach we buy her special tins of food because the dried cat food has yeast in it. On Shabbat we often give her a special food treat.

Sarah

## Achieving a balance

Jews, like everyone else, often find themselves facing dilemmas. On the one hand, they have the teachings in the Torah and, on the other, their own wishes and needs. It can often seem like a balancing act. Below are a few things that need balancing. Choose *one* of these issues and give your own views on it. Give at least *two* reasons for your opinion.

- Animals must be cared for but meat is good to eat and needs to be affordable. Factory farming is an efficient way of producing meat to eat.
- Everybody wants to live in good housing but trees must not be cut down.
- Nuclear power can provide cheap electricity but nuclear waste has to be disposed of.

**Activity**

2 With a partner, consider how Sooty should be cared for. Bear in mind the teaching on pages 50–51.

3 Since Sooty lives in the home of an Orthodox Jewish family, are there any other things you think would have to be kept in mind when feeding her?

4 Many Jews are as concerned as non-Jews about caring for the planet. Design a leaflet that could be given out in a kosher supermarket to help shoppers think green when they shop.

5 Do you think the Torah would permit the use of animals for experiments relating to cosmetics? Why?

**C**

# The Noah Project

## Green celebrations

The Noah Project says: 'By taking into the ark the animals and birds, Noah's God-given mission was to save the earth's biodiversity from destruction.' To help make Jews more aware of green issues, the Noah Project has linked some of the Jewish festivals like Sukkot, **Shavuot** and **Tu B'Shvat** to care of the earth. They have prepared special study packs and encouraged people to donate to environmental projects during these festivals.

In 2000, at the start of the new millennium, synagogues from all branches of Judaism united to hold an Environmental Awareness Shabbat, called by its Hebrew name Shabbat Noach. It was so successful, that the idea continued for the next few years. Special sermons were given in the synagogue, leaflets were distributed and articles appeared in the Jewish press. They were designed not only to make Jewish people consider their actions and the effects they might have on the planet, but also to suggest more environmentally-friendly ways of going about their daily lives.

**THE NOAH PROJECT**

**Jewish Education, Celebration and Action for the Earth**

**A** The Noah Project is a Jewish environmental group in the UK. It began when some people met together to protest about the building of a by-pass in Berkshire that would destroy ancient woodland and areas of special scientific interest.

**Activity**

1 Why do you think Noah was chosen for the name of the Noah Project? You can check the details of Noah's story in Genesis 7.

2 The Noah Project gives around 10% of its profits to environmental tzedakah projects. How does this fit in with Jewish teachings about charity? Pages 44–45 will help you.

3 Find out about the festivals of Shavuot and Tu B'Shvat. How can they be linked to concern for the environment?

**B** These volunteers are putting their ecological beliefs into practice.

### objective

to examine a case study of the way an organisation puts Jewish teachings about the environment into practice

### glossary

Chametz
Shavuot
Tu B'Shvat

Trees have always been important in Judaism. Where there is a tree, there is water, a wise person said. The tree of life is a well-known image; the tree of knowledge in the Garden of Eden is another. When we talk of family trees, we once again recognise the strength of trees.

The Noah Project works to raise awareness of the importance of trees to the planet. Guided nature walks at festival time are one way. Members are not afraid of getting their hands dirty. Some have worked with the British Trust for Conservation Volunteers to clear the site of an ancient monument so more light can get in. This, in turn, improves the range of plants and butterflies.

## Pesach

One particular area that the Noah Project has campaigned about concerns Pesach. As part of the preparations for this most important festival, Jews clean their houses of **chametz** (yeast). It is traditional to put away all the usual crockery and cutlery and take out special sets for Pesach. These have been kept free of chametz. In the past, people often kept a special set to use during the festival but, with today's busy lifestyles, it has become convenient to use plastic cutlery and disposable paper plates.

Can you see any problem with this?

The Noah Project says that Jews, as members of the human race, should think about the effect on the planet that all their polystyrene cups, plastic plates and tinfoil cooking dishes that are dumped in landfill sites are having once Pesach is over. These are products which will not biodegrade and, worse, many contain chemicals that actually pollute the earth.

Members of the Noah Project say Pesach is a celebration of freedom, and Jews should demonstrate by their lifestyle that they are worth the freedom God has granted them.

Why might a special sealed packet of cutlery like this be necessary at Pesach? Why would the use of plastic cutlery concern members of the Noah Project?

**Activity**

4  Produce a leaflet the Noah Project could use at Pesach. It needs to explain what Jews can do to care for the earth. Use biblical teachings to support your point. Jewish families will need suggestions about what they can do that is kind to the planet, yet still keep to the rules.

5  The Noah Project is considering an Eco-kosher certificate for foods that have been produced without harming the planet. Many will be organic. Name *five* foods you would recommend for their certificate.

6  Design a logo for ecologically-friendly products that have been specially produced for Pesach. Keep in mind the special kosher requirements of Pesach.

# Shalom!

Many passages in Jewish scriptures point to peace as something all Jews should aim towards. Peace in their personal life as well as their national life.

**A** The word '**Shalom**' is a standard Jewish greeting and means peace. The decoration on this plate supports that idea with symbols to show how the land flourishes when there is peace. What symbols can you identify?

**B**

'Everyone will live in peace among his own vineyards and fig trees, and no one will make him afraid. The Lord Almighty has promised this.'

(Micah 4:4)

'[God] will settle disputes among great nations. They will hammer their swords into ploughs and their spears into pruning knives. Nations will never again go to war, never prepare for battle again.'

(Isaiah 2:4)

'The world stands on three things, on justice, on truth and on peace.'

(Ethics of the Fathers)

The great Rabbi Hillel said:

'Be of the disciples of Aaron, loving peace and pursuing peace.'

King Solomon said:

'Getting involved in an argument that is none of your business is like going down the street and grabbing a dog by the ears.'

(Proverbs 26:17)

'In God's eyes the man stands high who makes peace between men – between husband and wife, between parents and children, between management and labour, between neighbour and neighbour. But he stands highest who establishes peace among nations.'

(The Talmud)

Activity

1  Choose *one* of the passages in **B** and explain fully what it means.

2  Would any of the teachings in **B** be helpful in resolving an incident of bullying in the classroom? Why?

## Ideal peace in an ideal world

You might have noticed that the two prophets quoted in **B** were talking of peace in the future tense. This is because they were looking forward to the **Messianic Age**. Some time in the future, Jews believe God will send the **Messiah** to begin a new age on the earth. Orthodox Jews believe that the Messiah will be a real person sent to earth by God. Liberal and Reform Jews do not take the prophecies in the **Tenakh** literally but they look forward to a time when humanity will work together in peace.

### objective

to understand Jewish teachings about peace and conflict

### glossary

Messiah
Messianic Age
Milchemet mitzvah
Milchemet reshut
Pacifist
Shalom
Talmud
Tenakh
Vendetta

All branches of Judaism recognise that, at present, we are living in an imperfect world; whilst we should aim for peace, there are times when we have to accept that peace is impossible. The scriptures state there are times when war is necessary. Jews are told they have a duty to protect themselves, other Jews and those who are weak. It is also permitted for Jews to go to war to help another country, if that will prevent war spreading.

The writer of the book of Ecclesiastes said:

'Everything that happens in this world happens at the time God chooses… He sets the time for love and the time for hate, the time for war and the time for peace.'

(Ecclesiastes 3:1 and 8)

The Torah teaches Jews not to be **pacifists** and contains accounts of God commanding the Jews to go into battle, like the famous story in the book of Joshua. The **Talmud** has no hesitation in advising, 'If someone comes to kill you, kill him first.'

# The just war

The Torah says all able-bodied men are expected to serve in the army, with the exceptions of priests and the newly wed. In Israel today, this has been translated into compulsory military service for all young people, male and female.

Biblical teachings lead Jews to believe that two types of wars are permitted:

1 An obligatory war, a **milchemet mitzvah**. This may be one commanded by God or a war in self-defence.
2 An optional war, a **milchemet reshut**. This is a war fought to prevent someone attacking you. It also includes going to war to defend another country or to stop a war spreading.

Strict rules were laid down in the Torah about waging wars to prevent them turning into **vendettas** that went on endlessly and destructively. When the Torah stated:

'The punishment shall be life for life, eye for eye, tooth for tooth, hand for hand, foot for foot, burn for burn, wound for wound, bruise for bruise'

(Exodus 21:23–25)

it meant revenge is to be limited to exactly the same wrong.

3 Is it right to fight for peace? Debate this as a class and take a vote at the end.

4 Choose *one* of the soldiers in photo C. Write the script for a conversation between that person and a pacifist who says, 'Violence just breeds violence'.

C Modern Israel has been involved in many conflicts since it began. These have been in defence of their land, they argue. Would this be an acceptable biblical reason?

# Looking for peace

**A** This memorial is at Beth Shalom, a British Holocaust centre. What ideas has the sculptor used to remember the six million victims? How has the **menorah**, the Jewish candelabra, been incorporated?

## Peace in the home

Because home is at the heart of Judaism, it is a place where everyone can play their part in resolving conflicts. Rabbi Gamaliel taught that:

*He who makes peace in his house, it is as if he made peace in all of Israel. But he who brings jealousy and strife to his house, it is as if he brought them among all Israel.*

To try and create peace and harmony in an Orthodox home, members often accept traditional family responsibilities like those studied on pages 30–31.

Judaism does accept, however, that not all marriages work out as the couple hoped and, for this reason, divorce is accepted. It should be a last resort after the couple has tried hard to resolve their differences.

'The law of divorce is given for the sake of peace. And those that divorce when they must, bring good upon themselves, not evil,' said a wise rabbi.

If the couple has been granted a divorce by the **Bet Din** (see pages 12–13), they are free to marry again and no slur is attached to a divorcee in Judaism.

## Peace in the community

'Work for peace within your household, then in your street, then in your town,' a rabbi told his followers.

It is said that when Moses' brother, Aaron, wanted to make peace between two people who were quarrelling, he would approach each privately without the other's knowledge. He told each one that the other person was sorry for upsetting them and wanted to settle their differences. This meant that when the protagonists next met they immediately patched things up.

**Activity**

1 Do you think it creates a peaceful family if everyone has set duties? Why?

2 a Make a note of the arguments for and against divorce.

   b What did the rabbi mean when he said divorce brought good, not evil, on the couple involved? Would you agree with this? Why?

3 Write a modern-day story that successfully uses Aaron's technique for settling arguments. Do you think it might work in reality? Why?

# Never again!

The murder of six million Jews in the Second World War was the worst massacre of Jews in history. A third of the Jewish population of the world was wiped out by Hitler. Jews know that it is vital these people are not forgotten. Keeping alive their memory is proof that evil did not ultimately win. Jews and non-Jews alike believe that remembering the **Holocaust** will help to prevent such horrific actions from occurring again. Holocaust remembrance can be a force for peace.

The Jewish calendar sets **Yom Hashoah**, or Holocaust Day, aside to remember those who perished. In Israel, everything closes down that day and many Jews attend synagogue. In Britain, Jewish families light a memorial candle at home for those who died and most families did lose relatives.

In January 2000, an annual Holocaust Remembrance Day was set up in Britain for Jews and non-Jews to commemorate those who died at the hands of the Nazis. Special exhibitions and education programmes have begun to take place around this time and it is hoped the memory of the Holocaust will promote international peace.

A special Holocaust Memorial Park was set up some time ago in Israel at Yad Vashem near Jerusalem. It commemorates those who died in the concentration camps and have no grave. Yad Vashem has also become the centre for worldwide Holocaust studies and, as the Chief Rabbi explains, all of this looks forward as much as it looks backward.

**B** This is Yad Vashem's memorial to the 1.5 million babies and children who were murdered during the Holocaust. Look closely at the way the figure and the wire have been drawn. What feeling does this memorial give you?

> We don't remember for the sake of the past but for the sake of the future. So that if we again see people deprived of rights, driven from their homes, dispossessed and crying for help, we don't stand still and do nothing. People who forget the past... are destined to repeat it. And there are certain things we just can't let happen again.
>
> (Chief Rabbi)

**Activity**

4 Explain why the Chief Rabbi thinks it is important to remember the Holocaust?

5 Beth Shalom means 'house of peace'. Research how this British Holocaust centre is working towards peace. Give a presentation of your research to the class.

# Reaching out for peace

## objective

to look at the ways Jewish interfaith activities promote peace

## glossary

Interfaith
People of the Book

**A** Jeremy Michelson, far right and an author of this book, welcomes Muslim visitors to the Manchester Jewish Museum. Members of the local mosque had previously welcomed Jewish visitors to their place of worship.

## Salaam–Shalom

'Hands across the religious divide' was how the *Manchester Evening News* headlined their report on local Jewish and Muslim activities to promote good relations. The idea came out of a chance meeting between a Jewish solicitor and a Muslim teacher. Both wanted to improve the understanding between their two communities and this led to an invitation to visit the mosque. 'They were so welcoming and even gave us kosher food, so we thought we'd do the same for them,' one of the Jewish visitors said. The Manchester Jewish Museum was chosen as the most appropriate venue for the return visit because this beautiful old building had once been a synagogue. Downstairs it still looks like a synagogue but upstairs there are lots of exhibits to help people understand Judaism. Jeremy Michelson, the museum's education officer and an author of this book, gave a talk to the Muslim visitors. After the visitors were given a tour of the building, they were given the chance to see and examine sacred objects for themselves, as well as ask questions and taste Jewish hospitality!

One significant thing to come out of the visits was that both Jews and Muslims realised how much they had in common.

1  What aspects of photo **A** are surprising? Why?

2  Imagine you run an advertising agency and have been employed by Salaam–Shalom to promote Jewish and Muslim interfaith activities.

   a  Write a mission statement that sets out the aims of this organisation.

   b  Design a logo and some merchandise they could sell to raise money for their work. This might be a pen, mug, or T-shirt, or you could include your own ideas.

3  Investigate the common ground between Jews and Muslims. Areas you might like to begin researching could be Abraham and Ibrahim; family life and the role of women; or dietary rules. You could give a three-minute presentation to the class or produce a poster called: 'The **People of the Book**'.

# Kicking out conflict

Getting young boys together to play football proved such a success that the enterprise, which is an initiative and programme of the Maimonides Foundation, was reported in the national papers and even featured on television. A hundred and twenty children aged between 9 and 12 get together in mixed-faith teams to play football on three Sundays. What has made it even more successful is that Arsenal Football Club offered to help with the training and their goalkeeper presented certificates to those who took part.

The project has brought together Jews and Muslims. It has also brought together Jews from various branches like Orthodox, Liberal and Reform congregations, and Muslims from Pakistan, Bangladesh, Turkey and Africa. Parents who bring their children often stay and watch, which has led to the adults also getting to know each other better.

**C**  The logo of the Maimonides Foundation shows the title of one of Moses Maimonides' books, *The Guide for the Perplexed*, written in Arabic, English and Hebrew.

**THE MAIMONIDES FOUNDATION**
*Harmony through dialogue*

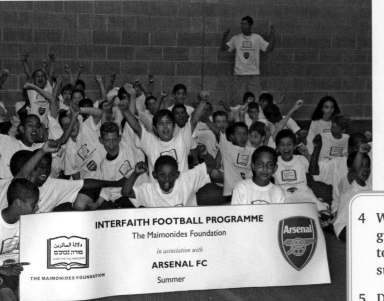

INTERFAITH FOOTBALL PROGRAMME
The Maimonides Foundation
*in association with*
**ARSENAL FC**
Summer

**B**  This is a successful **interfaith** activity in London. The group here were photographed in 2005, but the project actually began towards the end of the twentieth century.

4  Why do you think football was chosen for a group activity? Do you think it would appeal to girls as well? If not, what would you suggest as an activity to unite girls?

5  Design an A4 folded leaflet for The Maimonides Foundation to distribute to schools. It needs to explain what the Foundation is doing and why. It must also say who is eligible to take part and the good things that could come from being involved in this project.

6  Research sufficient information about Moses Maimonides to write a short article about him. Don't forget to use pages 44 and 45.

# Assessment for Unit 3

'So God created human beings, making them to be like himself. He created them male and female, blessed them, and said, "Have many children, so that your descendants will live all over the earth and bring it under their control. I am putting you in charge of the fish, the birds, and all the wild animals."'

(Genesis 1:27–28)

These questions test different sets of skills in RE. Which skills do you need to work on? Choose the level you need and work through the tasks set.

## Level 3

- Read the extract from Genesis above. Which part could a Jewish person quote to show that God has given them the right to rule over animals? Do you think we have the right to use animals as we like? Why?
- Describe *two* different kinds of war that a Jewish country is allowed to fight. What would your reaction be if you were called up to fight? Why?
- Describe *three* ways that Jews put the Torah teachings about caring for the poor into action. What is your response to the person collecting for charity outside the supermarket? Why?

## Level 4

- Describe what Jewish people mean when they speak of being 'stewards of the earth'. What difference could it make to the way they behave? Do you think it is worth doing? Why?
- Is it possible, according to the Torah, for a Jew to be a pacifist? If not, why not?
- In Judaism there is an idea called 'Tikkun Olam – Mending the World'. How have Jewish charities like World Jewish Relief and Tzedek put this idea into practice? Why do you think that non-Jewish organisations like Barnardo's still want to help people?

## Level 5

- What difference would it make to the welfare of the cow in the picture if the farmer was Jewish? What biblical teachings would inspire him?
- Is it acceptable for a Jewish person to be a pacifist, or does everyone have a duty to fight for his/her country?
- Read the extract from Deuteronomy 15:1 on page 45. What does this tell us about the Jewish attitude to poverty? How practical is this for today's society?

## Level 6

- What would your reaction be to some Jewish people who might say that helping to combat poverty and homelessness is less important than concentrating on personal spiritual development, and that the difficult world problems should be left to others?
- How far can the extract from Genesis be seen to contradict the idea in the Torah that we must be kind to animals?
- The Torah encourages man to 'conquer' the planet. What environmental challenges face the observant Jew who takes this command literally? Explain how the concept of stewardship fits in with this. Do you think that a non-believer has any responsibility towards the environment? Why?

# Glossary

**Anti-Semitism**   Being prejudiced against Jews on account of their religion.

**Ark**   Cupboard that holds the Torah scrolls in the holiest part of the synagogue.

**Bar Mitzvah**   Means 'son of the commandments' and is a ceremony when a 13-year-old Jewish boy takes responsibility for his religious life, it marks him becoming a man.

**Bat Chayil**   Means 'daughter of worth' and is a ceremony for a 12-year-old Orthodox Jewish girl that marks her undertaking full religious responsibility.

**Bet Din**   (Beth Din) A court of three rabbis who judge what is correct according to Jewish law.

**Bimah**   The reading desk for the scrolls in a synagogue.

**Chametz**   Crumbs of yeast that must be cleared away before Pesach starts.

**Covenant**   An agreement between God and the Jewish people.

**Creator**   Jews believe God made the heavens, the earth and everything that exists out of nothing.

**Fallow**   A field left unsown to rest the land.

**Free will**   The idea that people can choose how they behave.

**Gemach**   A group that lends something needed for a special occasion in return for a donation.

**Halakhah**   The Jewish law based on the Torah.

**Holocaust**   The racial attack on Jews by the Nazis between 1933 and 1945, which killed six million Jews.

**Interfaith**   When Jews and other faiths work together.

**Islamaphobia**   Being prejudiced against Muslims on account of their religion.

**Ketuvim**   The 3rd section of the Hebrew Bible, which contains sacred writings such as the Psalms.

**Kippah**   A skull cap worn by Jewish boys and men as a sign of respect for God.

**Kosher**   (Also 'Kashrut'.) Means right or correct for Jews to use.

**Laws of Kashrut**   (Also kosher) They describe what is right for a Jew to eat.

**Liberal Jew**   Believes the details of Jewish observance are less important than keeping to the spirit of Judaism.

**Mantle**   The decorated cover over a scroll in the synagogue.

**Matriarch**   The four founding mothers of Judaism: Sarah, wife of Abraham; Rebecca, wife of Isaac; Leah and Rachel, the wives of Jacob.

**Matzah**   Bread made without yeast for use throughout Pesach.

**Menorah**   Seven-branched candlestick which is an important symbol of Judaism.

**Messiah**   A spiritual leader God will send to earth in the future to lead Jews into a time of peace.

**Messianic Age**   A time in the future when Jews believe there will be a God-given period of peace on the earth.

**Mezuzah**   A parchment scroll containing the Shema prayer inside a case that is fixed to the right-hand side of a doorpost.

**Milchemet mitzvah**   An obligatory war commanded by God for self-defence.

**Milchemet reshut**   An optional war which might be started to prevent a worse situation happening.

**Minyan**   A group of 10 adult males who must be present for full synagogue worship to take place.

**Mishnah**   A collection of writings given to Moses by God that help Jews to interpret the Torah.

**Mitzvah (Mitzvot** = plural**)**   A God-given commandment or rule which Jews must obey.

**Moses Maimonides**   One of the greatest Jewish philosophers, Rabbi Moshe ben Maimon, 1135–1204 CE.

**Nevi'im**   The 2nd part of the Hebrew Bible, which contains writings by the Prophets.

**Noahide Laws**   The seven basic rules of living God gave to Noah.

**Oral Torah**   Parts of the scripture God gave to Moses and handed down by word of mouth before being written.

**Orthodox Jew**   Believes the Torah is the word of God and they should live their lives as close to the Torah rules as possible.

**Pacifist**   Someone who is against war and believes conflicts should be settled peacefully.

**Patriarch**   One of the three founding fathers of Judaism: Abraham; Isaac; and Jacob.

**People of the Book**   Jews, Christians and Muslims are called this because they hold similar scriptures sacred.

**Pesach**   (Passover) Eight-day festival that celebrates the Jews' freedom from slavery.

**Prophet**   A messenger from God.

**Pushke**   A small charity collecting tin found in a Jewish home.

**Rabbi**   Teacher in the Jewish community and synagogue.

**Reform Jew**   Believes Judaism is a living religion that should move with the times.

**Reincarnation**   Belief that when a person dies their soul is reborn into a new body.

**Resurrection**   The belief that Jesus rose from death, as in Christianity.

**Rosh Hashanah**   Jewish New Year which lasts two days and begins the 10 days of repentance.

**Sefer Torah**   The scroll that contains the handwritten text of the Torah scriptures.

**Shabbat**   The Jewish day of rest from sunset Friday until nightfall Saturday.

**Shalom**   The Hebrew word for peace. It is also a greeting.

**Shavuot**   A harvest festival that celebrates the giving of the Torah to Moses.

**Shema**   Most important Jewish prayer that states the basic belief in one God.

**Shochet**   Jewish butcher trained in the kosher method of slaughter.

**Shuir**   A study session.

**Stewardship**   The idea that humans look after the earth for God.

**Sukkah**   A simple hut Jews construct in which to celebrate Sukkot.

**Sukkot**   The festival of tabernacles which has a harvest theme.

**Synagogue**   Means 'meeting place' and is the place Jews meet to worship and study and for social events.

**Tallit**   A fringed shawl worn by Jewish men and some Reform women for prayer.

**Talmud**   Often called the 'oral Torah' because it was handed down by word of mouth.

**Taslich**   Ceremony at New Year to symbolise the casting away of sins.

**Tefillin**   Leather boxes containing the Shema, attached by straps and worn on the head and arm by a Jewish man for prayer.

**Ten Commandments**   Rules handed down by God to Moses.

**Tenakh**   The name of the Hebrew Bible.

**Teshuvah**   Means repentance – saying you are sorry for what you have done and promising never to repeat the sin.

**Torah**   Means the laws or teachings, the first five books of the Bible.

**Tu B'Shvat**   Spring festival in Israel when Jews plant trees to show respect for God's creation.

**Tzedakah (**or **Tzedaka)**   Hebrew for charity. A Jew should donate 10% of their income to the poor.

**Tzedek**   Means justice and righteousness.

**Vendetta**   Attacks of aggression that have no end because each side insists on 'paying back' the other.

**Yeshiva**   A college for higher Jewish studies.

**Yom Hashoah**   Hebrew name for Holocaust Day.

**Yom Kippur**   The Day of Atonement, the last of the 10 days of repentance and the holiest day of the year.

**Yom Tov**   A festive day in which work is forbidden.

# Index